THE
BIG BOOK
OF DAN

*Road Alligators and Other
Incongruous Possibilities*

Happy Reading

Dan Quetel

THE
BIG BOOK
OF DAN

*Road Alligators and Other
Incongruous Possibilities*

DANIEL C. DULIK

outskirts
press

Denver, Colorado

The opinions expressed in this manuscript are solely the opinions of the author and do not represent the opinions or thoughts of the publisher. The author has represented and warranted full ownership and/or legal right to publish all the materials in this book.

The Big Book of Dan
Road Alligators and Incongruous Possibilities
All Rights Reserved.
Copyright © 2012 Daniel C. Dulik
v3.0

Cover Photo © 2012 JupiterImages Corporation. All rights reserved - used with permission.

This book may not be reproduced, transmitted, or stored in whole or in part by any means, including graphic, electronic, or mechanical without the express written consent of the publisher except in the case of brief quotations embodied in critical articles and reviews.

Outskirts Press, Inc.
http://www.outskirtspress.com

ISBN: 978-1-4327-7859-0

Outskirts Press and the "OP" logo are trademarks belonging to Outskirts Press, Inc.

PRINTED IN THE UNITED STATES OF AMERICA

Contents

A Writer's Life 1

Acronym (A Folly) 3

Revealed 13

The Evolution of Man 15

Ego 33

People Who Need People? 35

The Narcissist 51

I Survived! Or Did I? 53

Integrity 61

The Consolidated "I" 63

Nose Hairs 71

Berm Bingo 73
    Introduction – The Game: How It Came About 73
    Chapter 1: The Roundabout Origins of Berm Bingo 73
    Chapter 2: Rules of the Game 83
    Chapter 3: Scoring 87
    Chapter 4: Road Alligators 93

The Highway
    (As It Has Replaced the River in the Human Psyche) 103

At the Off Ramp (Or the Homogenization of Our Society) 115

Tennessee Driving Philosophies and Practices 123

Rolling Down a Hill 131

More, More, More: People Need Less More and More Less 133

Is Reason Gone Forever? 143

What Are We About?	145
Point/Counterpoint	159
A Dispute Over Price?	161
Daylight Savings Time	171
Life at Both Ends	175
Patty Fatty and the Hunchback, Cha Cha Cha	179
Philandering	189
Bubba and Me	191
Getting Old	201
A View from the Bottom	219
Growing in Age	221
I Want to Go Low and Slow	223
Tom – My Remembrance	225
This Nose of Killer Man Jaro	235
What Are Words Worth, Longfellow?	237

A Writer's Life

Read it through:

Conceiving with jubilation
Writing with exhilaration
Editing with hesitation
Submitting with trepidation
Waiting with anticipation
Hoping for adulation
Praying for remuneration
Reading with dejection
Noting a new rejection
Contemplating with introspection

Start at top, begin anew:

Acronym (A Folly)

IN A TIME long, long away, in a land far, far ago, deep in the bowels of a building removed from the bustle of the central city, there existed a committee whose charter was formed under a directive named the *Aggregate Congressional Re-engineering of Natural Yard Mammals*, or *ACRONYM*. The Scientific Bureau of the Department of Agriculture, in the process of perfecting a sophisticated new genetic engineering technique, originated this directive. Once various committees defined all the parameters for all the targeted species, the genetic re-engineering work could begin. Charged with the redesigning of farm animals, one committee's task was to bring them up to government standards.

Made up of senior career politicians, the committee's goal included continuing to act as politicians. They realized that, being first in line, if the plan went sour they would be cast in a bad light. To avoid this, the committee members appointed a subcommittee of junior political rivals to deflect repercussions of the *ACRONYM* directive. Being more than astute adversaries, the members of the subcommittee knew it necessary to deflect blame for adverse outcomes from themselves; therefore, they conceived their own sub-subcommittee.

Commissioning this new sub-subcommittee by the subcommittee, which was charged by the committee to commission such a sub-subcommittee, presented a rather confusing circumstance. To clarify the sub-subcommittee's mission and bestow a name befitting their purpose, the sub-subcommittee heretofore would be titled the *Environmental Interlarding Ecosystem Interloping Organization*, or the EIEIO. It was further decided in committee by the subcommittee that the members of the newly instituted sub-subcommittee would be recruited from the private sector, which would further distance itself from the outcome of the new *Aggregate Congressional Re-engineering* of *Natural Yard Mammals* and the workings of the *Environmental Interlarding Ecosystem Interloping Organization*.

The first successful candidate hired was Bob Haypenny. Bob spent 30 years in a major accountancy in London that only handled transactions large enough to be accounted in pounds sterling. Yearning for change, he moved to the United States. The insatiable urge to account for the smallest amount or to dote on the smallest detail defined his nature. He soon found employment, splitting his time between the *Penny Saver* publication and the *Thrifty Nickel*. Later, he successfully obtained employment with the *Coinstar Company*, accounting for all the change in their machines. Although challenged by his work, he found no solace in change accounting and decided to cash it in and move on. This is how he came to be hired by the subcommittee of the committee to work in the sub-subcommittee known as the *EIEIO*.

Bob presented a contradiction of physical attributes. His massive chest formed an exaggerated inverted triangle from the base of a squat stump of a nearly indistinguishable neck all the way to his belt line. His arms boasted powerful, large biceps connected, curiously, to spindly forearms and unexpectedly tiny hands. From his belt line down lay an entirely different configuration, similar to that of a male ballet dancer. A thin waist with protruding, rounded buttocks and sparse but muscular legs, oddly short for the size of his upper torso, gave him an unusual but entertaining prancing gait. Atop the stump of neck, creased by fatty skin that extending far into the hairline, sat a round, basketball-sized head.

Bob's face could only be called loveably ugly. He had a heavily jowled mouth, and folds of skin rolled down his cheeks and forehead. In times of joy or severe stress, his tongue might protrude from the left side of his mouth, along with a thin stream of drool.

The subcommittee had the impression from the very first interview that Bob Haypenny was a person who could get his teeth into a problem and doggedly pursue it until he was satisfied with the solution. They were euphoric when Bob agreed to join as the first member of the *Environmental Interlarding Ecosystem Interloping Organization*.

ACRONYM (A FOLLY)

The next prospect the subcommittee approached was an adjunct English professor. Mrs. Kama Hyfa-Nader was seeking gainful employment after her professorship had been twice made redundant. Her employment had been parenthetically punctuated by a long absence resulting from a forced convalescence. She had been on holiday in India for two months during the summer recess and suffered a mishap with her gear while SCUBA diving in the Bay of Bengal. As a common prank, the Hindi guides often put a small amount of helium in tourists' air tanks so they would scream like angry munchkins when they rose to the surface and found the dive boat had been moved. On a rare occasion, the prank would turn sour, and unfortunately, this was just such an occasion for Kama Hyfa-Nader. She ingested a large bubble of helium that moved rapidly into her small intestine and then her descending colon, causing immediate distress. She ascended at a rate exceeding recommended practice, which caused the bubble to expand. This large helium bubble led to a condition, similar to the bends, called Diverticklelightass, named both for a sensation felt in the lower reaches of the body as well as a feeling of near weightlessness from the trapped helium. If left untreated, Diverticklelightass could cause one to tiptoe all the time. In extreme cases, for people who either could not afford treatment or who for health reasons could not undergo surgery, this could cause disastrous results. There were reported cases of people having to carry heavy weights, tethered at the ankles, for their entire lives. One man in Bangladesh went out on a windy day and high air currents carried him away. Luckily, remembering a teaching of his Yogi on the duality of the sphincters, he belched and farted his way to a soft landing in Venezuela.

Kama Hyfa-Nader fortunately did not suffer these fates. She had an uncle, a world-renowned proctologist, by her side. He would do anything for his favorite niece. He was enamored of her and even named one of his most perfected techniques after her. It was the Kama suture. He performed a successful operation in record time to relieve the pain and suffering of poor Kama. Part of her colon had to be removed since the damage was more extensive than originally thought. He used his signature technique of the Kama suture, but after completed, she was left with a semicolon and a long recovery period.

The subcommittee, enthralled with the prospect of hiring Kama Hyfa-Nader, enjoyed high spirits when she agreed to join the sub-subcommittee. Kama was not imposing; in fact, her physique was the antithesis of Bob's impressive hulk. Diminutive in stature, she bore spindly appendages and slender, smallish digits. Kama's facial features, in combination, were intriguingly familiar. She had a severely receding jaw line, a long pointed nose, and bulging brown eyes. Tan splotches and dark moles dotted her face, accentuating the overall skin tone of a brown paper bag. The quality most admired by the subcommittee, however, had nothing to do with her physical appearance. This quality was, more than likely, an outcome of her physical appearance and interaction with people. Kama's best quality was the relentless pursuit of her position in any argument. Her staccato cacophony of words, once mentally composed, was repeated endlessly, acknowledged or not. In social situations, she accosted each individual with her nagging views. Moving in rapid, nervous bursts from one person to another, she would iterate and reiterate with a diabolical resonance shrilly repulsive to the normal human ear. What a find! The subcommittee, energized by this discovery, immediately set out to acquire the third member of the *EIEIO*.

Born of parents too closely related to be husband and wife in most states, and both of whom were avid prime time TV aficionados, Starsky Ann Hutch suffered years of jocular prodding from friends and family. Even her brother, Rabbit, and sister, China, thought her name to be a target of jovial commentary. Her upbringing spurred Starsky's aspiration to become someone admired in society. With the name Starsky Ann Hutch, a career in law enforcement seemed a natural choice. She breezed through the police academy, received an appointment to the police force, and spent five boring years giving out parking tickets. In frustration over the lack of advancement, she quit. Star, as she was known, opened a detective agency in the central city doing mostly surveillance work for the *Agrarian Surveillance of Perverse Congressional Activity, or the ASPCA*.

ACRONYM (A FOLLY)

The subcommittee thought it would be of great benefit to have a person on the sub-subcommittee with experience as a public servant and an affiliation with the *ASPCA*. Had they realized that the *ASPCA* affiliation was not the *ASPCA they* were familiar with, the subcommittee may have realized they were about to plant a mole, and they could not have pointed to Star as a collaborator in the quest to accomplish the directive *Aggregate Congressional Re-engineering of Natural Yard Mammals*. Star Hutch was accepted and sworn in as the third member of the *Environmental Interlarding Ecosystem Interloping Organization*.

Star's demeanor, in one word, would be sleek, in two words, sleek and stealthy. Surveillance became the watchword of her business. She developed an uncanny ability to perceive the smallest of details. Hair bobbed and slicked back from an angular face, Star was tall and sinewy with well-defined musculature. Her irises were brilliant green orbs with slit-like pupils that, in low light, dilated to encompass most of the iris; this allowed her to catch nearly imperceptible activity. Brows that angled upward on either side of the nose bridge and then flared straight back to wrap slightly to the side of her face accentuated the attractive eyes. Nostrils of an impish pug flared above a wry smile, completing the look. Her walk was a study in fluid grace. She walked with chin high and jutted forward, like a runner stretching for the finish. Her long legs moved in a slinky fashion, and her arms undulated in synchronicity with her legs so that the overall appearance was one of liquid motion.

Starsky Ann Hutch became the third member of *EIEIO* and looked forward to participating in the activities of the sub-subcommittee (while secretly holding on to her affiliation with the *ASPCA*).

Approaching the end of the selection process, the committees, as well as the subcommittee, were anxious to find another person or two to round out the group. Because of this anxiety, the committee decided to direct the subcommittee to find only one more appointee. If the group could not reach consensus, they agreed, another member could be added to the mix later.

THE BIG BOOK OF DAN

Desperation more than ability helped them choose the fourth and final member of the sub-subcommittee. Although the candidate did exude electrifying exuberance, his qualifications were luminously lackluster. After graduation from Twolane University in an accelerated program with no breaks, he became an ambulance chaser. This, he realized, was not the life for him, but the ability to earn a living any other way seemed impossible considering his qualifications. Desperation drove Jack Russell to take the one talent he claimed and parlay it into a modest living and a touch of fame. Jack became a professional long distance runner, supported in his career by the Parklane Pantyhose Company. As Jack aged, his ability to perform as a runner hit more than one snag, but one attribute remained with him. His amiable nature endeared him to the executive committee of Parklane and left them wanting to give him a pat on the head and a graceful retirement from the demands of being a runner. This goal actualized when an executive of the company, big in plus size panty hose, was shoehorned into a Congressional seat ironically left vacant by a Congressman involved in a scandalous charge of transvestitism. Jack was appointed to the *EIEIO* directly by the committee that commissioned the subcommittee, which commissioned the *Environmental Interlarding Ecosystem Interloping Organization*.

With all of the committee members in place, the time arrived to begin proceedings with the redesign of farm animals in their province. The first assignment involved a rather timely redesign of a traditional beast of burden. In keeping with the movement toward "Green Power," which, by the way, historically occurs after periods of extreme overindulgence and anguished cries about dependence on foreign oil, the committee decided to come up with a new design for the *Highly Operable Readily Serviceable Equine,* or *HORSE*.

The first meeting was called to order in the offices of the *EIEIO* around the big round conference table. This meeting allowed for a "feeling out" process, each taking inventory of the other. Bob sat on the edge of his seat with his hands knuckled under, supporting the weight of his upper body. His head bounced and swiveled, eyes trying to fix on Kama, who was scurrying around the room, nervously inspecting all of the accoutrements placed for their convenience. Waiting for the festivities to begin, Star sat quietly coiled in her chair. Jack fetched donuts and coffee for all before jumping into his chair and sitting attentively, waiting for the first suggestion to be proffered. The meeting remained relatively uneventful. The members adopted a suggestion to model their meetings after those held by the committee that appointed the subcommittee that commissioned their sub-subcommittee. In this model, each person offered an idea, discussed its merits, and incorporated it into the plan. This appeared to be how committees operated, throwing in ideas and designs dear to each member until they had a finished product. All in agreement, the meeting was adjourned and a date set for the first working meeting.

The first working meeting was called. Each member described what he or she thought would be a good feature for the *Highly Operable Readily Serviceable Equine*. Then they would all nod in agreement, note the feature, incorporate it, and move on. This went swimmingly until noon, with all the ideas noted, the donuts and snacks consumed, and no further action needed. The meeting was adjourned. Star had the task of typing the minutes and the report. These documents were then submitted to the subcommittee for forwarding to the committee. She secretly sent a copy of the report, along with the designs, to her friends at the *Agrarian Surveillance of Perverse Congressional Activity*, who in turn forwarded it to the *Sanctimonious Avian Commandoes*, or *SAC*.

With great anticipation and expecting commendations all around, the *EIEIO* awaited word on their grand plan to redesign the *HORSE*. The subcommittee reviewed the report and forwarded it for further review to the committee, who then presented it to the Department of Agriculture's scientific branch. This branch immediately rejected the plan, sending it back to the committee, who sent it back to the subcommittee, who sent it back to the *Environmental Interlarding Ecosystem Interloping Organization* with the following notation:

◄ THE BIG BOOK OF DAN

Plan Rejected:

In review of the recommendations submitted regarding the re-design of the Highly Operable Readily Serviceable Equine, we find the outcome of your activity totally unacceptable. The computer model generated using all of these features appears to be what can only be described as a Catastrophic Amalgamated Multifunctional Egalitarian Landrover, or CAMEL, which would be totally unsuited to farm use.

The *EIEIO,* duly censured for their failure, received a warning that fur would fly if another disaster such as this occurred. Wanting to succeed, each member became more aggressive in fighting for ideas and fighting against everyone else's, in such a way that nothing ever got finished. The pressure was on to submit their plan for the *Portly Insatiable Glutton,* or *PIG,* by week's end. As the time grew near, in desperation they submitted a plan for adding a fifth leg to the beast to increase the Hams Per Hog, or *HPH* quotient. The plan was well received by the subcommittee and the committee until they both found out that an "ad hoc committee" had presented the original idea the previous session. During all of these goings on, Star secreted plans out of the sub-subcommittee and forwarded them to *Agrarian Surveillance of Perverse Congressional Activity,* who in turn forwarded them to the *Sanctimonious Avian Commandoes.*

Increasingly disenchanted with the output of the *EIEIO,* the committee put extreme pressure on the subcommittee to get the sub-subcommittee on track. Along with the upheaval over the non-performance of the *Environmental Interlarding Ecosystem Interloping Organization,* there were signs of growing distrust of the program, and threatening letters arrived alluding to the unleashing of violence and terror if the *ACRONYM* program continued. The *SAC* signed all the letters.

The general mood in the committee and subcommittee was that something needed to be done to elicit a win from the *EIEIO* on one

ACRONYM (A FOLLY)

hand and an investigation of the threats against the program on the other. To obtain the win so desperately needed, the subcommittee hired an addition to the sub-subcommittee, someone guaranteed to make things happen.

Lt. Colonel Pack Hunter U.S.M.C. (Retired) was added to the roster and soon became the prime mover of the organization. Pack Hunter rose to a challenge. He had trained the dogs of war on many occasions, teaching them to act as one unit toward a common goal. Tall, muscular, and solid in stature, he had steel gray eyes, an imposing growl for a voice, and a constant sneer in place of a smile. His hair was closely cropped and bristly. He was single minded, focused and mean. The members of the *EIEIO* got their first and last taste of Pack Hunter on the next meeting day.

In what turned out to be the last meeting, Pack was introduced to his charges, then he set forth his directives, and they began a "take no prisoners" march to their next goal. In record time, they developed a plan, completed the design, typed the minutes, and filed the report for what would be their final assignment. Thus, the *Saturday's Handy Embodiment of Ecstasy and Pleasure*, or the *SHEEP*, came into existence in just one meeting. Star filed all of the paper work with the subcommittee and secretly forwarded a copy to the *Agrarian Surveillance of Perverse Congressional Activity*, who in turn forwarded it to the *Sanctimonious Avian Commandoes*. The subcommittee dutifully forwarded the paperwork to the committee and so on up the line.

Even though the *Saturday's Handy Embodiment of Ecstasy and Pleasure* was a big hit with Congress, they immediately cancelled the program without explanation to the members of the *EIEIO*.

It would be some time before anyone knew the end of the story.

The *Federal Bureau of Investigation* or *FBI* initially investigated the threatening letters written by the *SAC*. The *FBI* warned Congress that if some members of the *SAC* had "gone rogue," they had control of enough nuclear firepower to wipe out the entire country. The *Strategic Air Command* was nothing to take lightly.

In truth, of course, the *SAC* that sent the letters was the *Sanctimonious Avian Commandoes,* a group of fanatic bird enthusiasts who believed that if the *Aggregate Congressional Re-engineering of Natural Yard Mammals* was successful, a program might be initiated to re-engineer their beloved bird species. When they became aware of the misunderstanding between the *Strategic Air Command* and the *Sanctimonious Avian Commandoes,* they decided to change not only their name but also their strategy for protesting government interference with the natural order of things. Whenever there was a perceived threat of any kind, they would come together dressed in their bright yellow Big Bird suits and erect and burn large wooden perches, chanting protests under their new name: the *CCC,* or *Coo Clucks Clan.*

Revealed

Swaddle me in truth.
Nurture me in wisdom.
Bathe me in joy.
Unclasp my pins.
Fold back my nappy
Cleanse me of all
that came before.

The Evolution of Man

WHEN IT CAME to finding a quotation on this subject, I was intrigued that so many people had something profound to say about the origin of the human species. So many of the things said had a different slant on us, modern creatures of this earth. It was too difficult to pick a quotation that could describe us or define us in a context that is similar to the way we define our surroundings, so I put in a varied selection.

While Darwinian Man, though well-behaved, At best is only a monkey shaved!

W. S. Gilbert (1836-1911), English librettist

It is curious how there seems to be an instinctive disgust in Man for his nearest ancestors and relations. If only Darwin could conscientiously have traced man back to the Elephant or the Lion or the Antelope, how much ridicule and prejudice would have been spared to the doctrine of Evolution.

Havelock Ellis (1859-1939), British psychologist.

It is disturbing to discover in oneself these curious revelations of the validity of the Darwinian theory. If it is true that we have sprung from the ape, there are occasions when my own spring appears not to have been very far.

Cornelia Otis Skinner (1901-79), U.S. author, actor.

The prehuman creature from which man evolved was unlike any other living thing in its malicious viciousness toward its own kind. . . . Humanization was not a leap forward but a groping toward survival.

> Eric Hoffer (1902-83), U.S. philosopher.

Organic life, we are told, has developed gradually from the protozoon to the philosopher, and this development, we are assured, is indubitably an advance. Unfortunately it is the philosopher, not the protozoon, who gives us this assurance.

> Bertrand Russell (1872-1970),
> British philosopher, mathematician.

I was taught that the human brain was the crowning glory of evolution so far, but I think it's a very poor scheme for survival.

> Kurt Vonnegut, Jr. (b. 1922), U.S. novelist.

What we think of as our sensitivity is only the higher evolution of terror in a poor dumb beast. We suffer for nothing. Our own death wish is our only real tragedy.

> Mario Puzo (b. 1920), U.S. novelist

THE EVOLUTION OF MAN

It is ironic that the one thing that all religions recognize as separating us from our creator-our very self-consciousness-is also the one thing that divides us from our fellow creatures. It was a bitter birthday present from evolution.

>Annie Dillard (b. 1945), U.S. author, poet.

We live between two worlds; we soar in the atmosphere; we creep upon the soil; we have the aspirations of creators and the propensities of quadrupeds. There can be but one explanation of this fact. We are passing from the animal into a higher form, and the drama of this planet is in its second act.

>W. Winwood Reade (1838-75), English traveler, author.

If the Lord Almighty had consulted me before embarking upon Creation, I should have recommended something simpler.

>Alfonso X King of Castile and Leon (1221-84)(attributed to). On hearing an explanation of the Ptolemaic system of astronomy.

And the Lord God formed man of the dust of the ground, and breathed into his nostrils the breath of life; and man became a living soul.

Bible, Hebrew . Genesis 2:7.

Why was the human race created? Or at least why wasn't something creditable created in place of it? God had His opportunity. He could have made a reputation. But no, He must commit this grotesque folly-a lark which must have cost Him a regret or two when He came to think it over & observe effects.

Mark Twain (1835-19101960).

Man was kreated a little lower than the angells and has bin gittin a little lower ever sinse.

Josh Billings [Henry Wheeler Shaw] (1818-85), U.S. humorist.

Back of every creation, supporting it like an arch, is faith. Enthusiasm is nothing: it comes and goes. But if one believes, then miracles occur.

Henry Miller (1891-1980), U.S. author.

Historians will have to face the fact that natural selection determined the evolution of cultures in the same manner as it did that of species.

Konrad Lorenz (1903-89), Austrian ethnologist.

If there is a God, and Adam and Eve were a reality, then as punishment for doubting him he threw them, not so much out of Paradise, but into Paradox as a constant state of being.

THE EVOLUTION OF MAN

On a recent trip from Knoxville, Tennessee (my new home) to Memphis, Tennessee (a place where I do business), I began thinking about a question that has been asked in every context from philosophical to physical since who knows when. This particular trip was in January, there were not too many dead animals on the berm to use for honing my gaming skills, not too many tourists to observe or to dodge, and so I spent most of the seven hours contemplating the enigma of the ages: where do we come from?

(I am inserting this essay at this time because I want to. It's my book, so I can; besides, if you look at why we *are*, you invariably ask *where we came from*.)

WHERE WE CAME FROM has two very different accepted schools of thought, Creationism and Evolutionism. I find neither very fulfilling and each with a larger list of unanswered questions than answered questions.

Since moving to Knoxville, I have become a social hermit to some degree, the reasons for which I will explain in a few chapters, but let's just say I don't get out much. Because I am prone to the prone position and few activities are possible from this position, I have become an avid watcher of the television, something I am not proud of but too fascinated with to change.

After watching so much TV, I have become rather jaded and developed definite preferences for certain types of programs. I am an avid fan of the 'ology' shows – anthropology, archeology, paleontology, cosmology, cosmetology (which is the study of the make-up of the earth), all of those 'ologies' that try to explain the origins of the earth and all the creatures that inhabit it. These shows are absolutely fascinating to me, not as much for content as for a great display of the ego of man in judging the world in which he lives.

All of the scientific guys that host these shows, or are interviewed on them, are stuck in this firm belief that what they think reality was a couple of million years ago has to be true. The glaring fact that strikes me is, they base their beliefs on what the world is today and run it backwards to tell you how animals ate, drank, lived, and died all those years ago. What bullshit this is. How the hell do they know the color of some lizard, or what it ate, or what its mating habits were, from a pile of bones? How can scientists state with such certainty what was going on millions of years ago with the evolution of animals? They don't even preface it with an "I think," or a "probably," and yet the battle still rages over the origin of man and his evolution, or lack of it.

For example, there is the Tyrannosaurus, the most talked about discovery in the world of paleontology since its bones were dug up. The fascination that we have with this particular creature may have a lot to do with the way we identify with the world. It is reported to have been a brutal, meat-eating creature. It was the brute of the forest killing all in its path. We admire brutal killing and mercilessness as good traits, so we are willing to accept any fable about these ancient animals as fact. These scientific guys prey on this predisposition of ours toward violence and postulate their theories based on our tendency to believe what they are saying. These science guys are regularly interviewed on the 'ology' shows with a computer-animated behemoth, resplendent in standard lizard brown and green, behind them. Certainly all of their assertions are based on how the world works today, but HOW THE HELL DO THEY REALLY KNOW that the world has always worked the same way? There are aberrations in our society, things that aren't as they seem to be, aren't there? Why could there not have been aberrations in the ancient world? Why do creatures from millions of years ago have to have behaved as animals do today? They don't have to! We shouldn't believe they do, or we are doomed. The fact that things never change is depressing. Are we doomed to live forever cast in a mold we cannot break?

On one of these 'ology' programs, some science guy was talking about the origin of the whale. The entire half hour was devoted to his theory that the whale was a land animal at one time and then returned to the ocean because it offered a more abundant food source. At one point in the show, he dragged out some bones and a rather fanciful drawing of this big wolf type creature and talked about how he had

THE EVOLUTION OF MAN

connected its evolutionary chain from a land roving wolf into a very different looking sea creature resembling a whale. Now, in looking at a wolf next to a whale, you would have to wonder how he made this connection. He presented a series of other skeletons with skin draped over them artistically to show this rather fanciful scenario from beginning to end. I bring up this point to launch us into the origins of man. Because if you can believe this to be true, then anything is possible from an evolutionary stand point, wouldn't you say?

Getting back to the origins of man, Creationists vs. Evolutionists, this is a battle not easily won because it deals in opinion and conjecture, and everyone is allowed to have an opinion based on what they think they know, or at least what they think they thought they knew. Perhaps it is time we examine the origin of man based on an entirely new approach, without the interference of logic or prejudice to hinder our mentalities.

The Creation theory always left an empty spot for me. It was never quite fulfilling. Perhaps this failing lies in how Creation supposedly worked. As I see it, a **POOF!** and an **OOPS!** were involved. First it was POOF!!! Here's ADAM!!... then it was OOPS!!! Here's EVE!

Now after looking over the timeline for this world of ours, we can see that man was a fairly recent invention. God had a long time to fool around with this process of creation and procreation using the animals as lab rats, so to speak. When He created us, He must have put great thought into it; after all, our egos tell us we are God's perfect creations. After ages of getting this procreation thing down, why did God just create Adam and then, as an afterthought, create Eve? Did God have the proverbial brain fart? Was this perhaps the male's way of forever keeping the female in check, by making her believe that she came from the male to begin with (the authors of the Bible were assumed to be male)? What was this rib thing,? Was God actually working on some type of cloning procedure? As you can see, professing a belief in God's Omnipotence and realizing His past experience in making animals just leaves a big nasty hole in the creation process as it pertains to humans.

Another aspect to consider is, who were Cain and Abel? With whom did they mate? Who were their partners in the furthering of the human species? Following the lineage of this rather restricted group, it would have to have been some very close relatives. Certainly God must have known about inbreeding and its ill effects on the continuation of a healthy species. Natural selection was at work for millions of years according to the 'ology' guys.

Creation as an explanation for our being here is not at all out of the question, but it does provide additional questions to be pondered, hence the emergence of the Theory of Evolution. Evolution being a viable alternative to creation is certainly acceptable. There is enough evidence to support evolution as a means for our being on the planet, but I find it as unsettling an explanation as creation.

On some other 'ology' program, a geneticist from some college somewhere (as you can tell the meat of the issue is always more important to me than the details) had traced the origins of man to one single female in Ethiopia or Uganda. This I also find suspicious; again only one half of the component of creation is being discussed As the Bible's authors were male and put the male as the originator of the species, this person was a female and put the female in as the only player in the game. She didn't say that there was any evidence of who the first male was. If scientists can prove what a lizard ate millions of years ago, how come they can't nail this one down, or at least offer a plausible explanation for this one-person phenomena?

The striking similarity is that one day, **POOF,** we just appeared as humans upon the earth, maybe a little hairier than today, but still, we appeared as humans to claim our rightful spot as masters of all we survey. Now how can that be? How can science on one hand tell us that whales came from wolves and then in the next breath tell us that we simply arrived? Scientists say, because we have many characteristics of the apes, that we probably came from apes. Now I have to ask, when did this transformation take place? Did some monkey get up one morning and put on a business suit or a dress and decide this was the day?

THE EVOLUTION OF MAN

If we descended from apes as claimed, and if we are so much better than apes, then why didn't all the apes decide to be people? This again is full of holes and does not leave me with any great confidence that we are farther along in our theories on the origin of man. For these reasons, I have postulated a theory that soothes the souls of both the Creationists and the Evolutionists, and I offer it to you as a reasonable explanation for the origin of man.

Forget the Creationists' **POOF** and **OOPS** and the Evolutionists' **Apes**. Those are false theories based on the functions of earthly creatures as we know them today. The worlds then and now, although similar, do not need to be the same and chances are they aren't.

In the great primordial ooze, every creature came from chemicals. Chemicals that were, for millions of years, fermenting. Any scientist will tell you we are nothing but chemicals. Each creature developed into a certain group of chemicals and eventually became a life form of one sort or another. One life form that has existed since creatures came out of the slime is the insect. Insects, then as now (don't forget all great scientists base then on now), had the ability to rapidly evolve to suit the needs of their surroundings They also had very short life spans, which allowed them to rapidly define their new forms and make revisions as needed. What if each insect had a poker-straight pattern of progress, so every creature ever alive could be traced back to its insect beginnings? This should include us; we must have come from some antediluvian insect species. We did have a lot of trouble accepting the COMING FROM MONKEYS THEORY, so this may be a little hard to swallow right this minute, but if you look at the fossils of the creatures that crawled out of the oceans and are claimed as the beginnings of life on earth, they are all insect-like in appearance, aren't they? If you accept evolution, you must accept the fact that we, at some time in our development, had to be bugs of one sort or another.

Accepting this as fact will help you understand how this whole thing works, so just believe it and we will continue.

One trait of many insects is the ability to reproduce without the customary mating of male and female. They have both male and female reproductive organs, or, as the 'ology' guys would say, "are hermaphroditic." This hermaphroditic characteristic is prevalent in some insects today and must have been more the rule than exception in a situation where life spontaneously evolved Anyway, let's just say that all creatures must have had this characteristic at some point in their beginnings.

If you consider our ancestors as a more primitive life form than the ancient ape-like creatures usually given credit, we must have had this characteristic at some point in our development. At some point in time, whatever we evolved from must have had the ability to reproduce without the customary ritual of dating and marriage and all of those unnatural acts we now subscribe to. This would of course be hard to prove for two reasons. The first is that all of the materials in question, being soft tissue, would have long ago rotted away. The second reason is man's natural need to romanticize about where we came from. The ego-based concept of our superior nature would not allow us to subscribe to a theory that we came from such low forms of life as bugs. Let's face it; if evolution is your belief, it had to have happened this way. We may have, in our ancestral tree, a cockroach or two.

The realization of our hermaphroditic beginnings explains every question our species has ever pondered about our beginnings, our development as a species, and the gender confusion we face at this point in our development. The big question now is, when in our timeline did we choose to split into the male and female components we are today? When did some of the species give up their male reproductive organs? When did the others choose to give up female reproductive organs? This is a troubling question that can't be answered in definite terms. We can, however, set the stage in which it could have happened with the same fanciful proficiency as the scientists that tell us how whales got to be whales.

Let's say that the human beings did not give up this trait until late in our development. Let's say that we were able to plop out little creatures on our own even after we started walking on our hind legs and

THE EVOLUTION OF MAN

had developed our front paws into hands with opposable thumbs. Let's say that at this point we were able to have litters of little creatures rather than just one or two as is normal today. Although we could spit them out at a rapid rate, there were too many animals around bigger, stronger, and more powerful than we were, gobbling offspring up as fast as we could produce them. Procreation of the species, being a powerful drive, kept us always in a state of gestation. It was too difficult to gather food and sustain ourselves in this condition. Let's also say that we as individuals were also beginning to recognize the existence of other like creatures in the same predicament. In an effort to solve our own personal dilemma, we began to associate with these other creatures, having bitch sessions over these problems and eventually deciding to band together in a common defense. This was the dawn of communal living.

We now have a communal colony of creatures all alike in physical traits, each having the ability to procreate little creatures on their own, each having the external genitalia of both sexes as well as the internal reproductive organs needed to make little creatures. For the first time social consciousness was required. Social consciousness began to take shape along with the physical arrangements necessary for this new evolutionary species to exist in a group.

As this group developed, it was as necessary as ever to take care of the physical needs of the individual along with all of the little creatures being produced. The founding premise of the society was protection of the little ones. Food gathering was a problem. Should they all go to find food, and if so, then all of the little creatures would be left unprotected from all of the other animals waiting in the bushes, waiting to eat all of those tasty little morsels lying around. A decision to divide the duties up among individuals must have occurred. This decision to divide and assign duties had to be the point at which civilization took a turn toward what we have today.

As it is today, there must have been differences in the abilities of individuals. Various tasks must have seemed more difficult to some than to others. The ability to reason and work out situations must have been easier for some than others. All animals have these abilities, as we are finally admitting, so let's assume this was true. The more intelligent of the species must have convinced the less mentally capable to do the food gathering chores. I am basing this determination on the fact that all of the creatures had the external genitalia of both sexes, and as fashion had not yet been invented, they must have all been naked. Judging by the fossil remains of the animals alive at the time and the size of their teeth, there were a lot of penises flopping around right at snout level in front of a bunch of very hungry animals. As they rooted through the bushes for suitable consumable items, they had to be very vulnerable. The food gatherers of this primitive group probably were not so smart to be talked into putting themselves in such peril.

We now have some semblance of a society with defined roles based on the mental abilities and persuasiveness of the individuals in the group. The smart ones got to stay behind to look after the little creatures while the dim-witted ones got to brave the ravages of a cruel world with their dicks dangling, bait for any hungry meat-eating creature out there. The unconscious memory of this perilous time stirs in every man. Each time a dog sniffs at his crotch, he will wince and swivel his hips, not wanting to expose himself to the danger of those sharp, unpredictable teeth.

The incidence of animal attack was very high to start with, and some of the food gatherers lost their external genitalia in these attacks. It did not take too many attacks to make the dimwitted ones realize the dangers of food gathering and to release in them an inordinate fear of having this same tragedy befall them. They became so afraid that they would only reluctantly go out to bring back the necessary food for the other members of the tribe. This fear even crept into their dreams, and sleep came fitfully to them. This lack of sleep further hampered their ability to gather food. Sleep deprivation caused them to become increasingly weak and nauseatingly whiny.

The smart ones could no longer control the situation, and something needed to be done. First, they needed to invent a way to allow

THE EVOLUTION OF MAN

the gatherers to rest comfortably without fear of the night creatures. This was the onslaught, although unwittingly, of sexual pairing. The smart ones decided to allow the dumb ones to hide their penises inside their vaginas, and the smart ones would stay awake during this period to ensure that no creatures could affect the feared act of biting off their penises while they slept. This worked well in the beginning. There was only one small hitch in the plan. The dumb ones began to like this new experience for reasons other than the intended purpose and did not want to sleep during the initial stages of hide-the-penis. Although their pleasure lasted only a few minutes, it was still troubling to the smart ones who were only doing it reluctantly as a means of keeping the dumb ones out there gathering the food needed to sustain the group. The smart ones tolerated the activity, the dumb ones would fall into a deep sleep afterward allowing them time to plan the next gathering excursion. This trait is prevalent even in today's 'highly developed society.'

Some very unexpected problems arose due to this new activity.

Among the gatherers, there were some who were more proficient than others. They became more prized to the non-gatherers than the ones who were not such good providers. They became coveted as the ones who could provide more for the ones waiting at home. They also were the ones who could most affect the food gathering process should they not get the needed sleep. They were given preferential treatment when it came time to hide their penises. Those with perceived special traits coveted by society are given preferential treatment. The perception is that they have the ability to pass these traits to their offspring. It is so ingrained into the subconscious that it is not realized, even when issue is not an issue. Some guys have all the luck, don't they?

Another problem that sprang up, so to speak, was the promulgation of small creatures from the hide-the-penis activity. Some correlation was noted between Hide the Penis and the impregnation of the non-gatherers. As each had the ability to conceive little creatures on their own, they knew they didn't cause a pregnancy, so it must have something to do with the newfound activity. This correlation between the sex act and the outcome of it is a problem even today and sometimes comes as quite a surprise to certain folks. As all of the previous little creatures could be attributed to just one adult, this new turn of events gave rise to addressing a set of more sophisticated social issues than previously addressed by the communal living arrangement. This must have been the beginnings of the arrangement we now know as the family, where one gatherer was responsible for the non-gatherer plus any of the offspring of the non-gatherer caused by the hide-the-penis activity.

A third problem was what to do with the poor unfortunates ravaged by beasts while gathering food for the group, and who had lost their penises in these savage attacks. Because they had also lost their beans (which testicles were called at that time), the term used for them was "Less Beans." The group shunned them since they were no longer complete individuals, and they were forced to seek out their existence in a group unto themselves. As a result of their isolation, they developed their own culture outside of the main group, and they eventually split off completely. Forming into a rather disgruntled, angry subgroup that made effigies of the heads of those who shunned them, they hit the heads around with big sticks, retrieved the heads, and let the one with the stick hit them again. Their hatred for the other group caused them not to want to be confused or identified with the other group, so they began wearing skins over their now disfigured bodies. These skins were their distinguishing trademark, identifying them from the hated group who had shunned them. Anthropologists believe this to be the rudimentary beginnings of softball as we know it today. Again, we are getting off track and should continue in the development of the mainstream social group.

As the custom of Hide the Penis became the norm rather than the exception, the evolution of today's human began. The dumb ones developed physical characteristics fitting to their activities. They became muscular and sinewy from repeatedly carrying heavy loads of groceries back to the waiting mob of smart ones and little creatures who were not yet able to provide for themselves. They lost the need to suckle their young and along with it their mammary glands. They eventually lost their female reproductive organs along with their outward female genitalia. While this was happening to the dumb ones, the smart ones were progressing in the exact opposite direction. They were shunning all of the characteristics no longer needed for a life of staying home. Their new forever and ever role would be taking care of the little creatures and deciding what to instruct the dumb ones to bring back from their next trip out, so why would they need all of those outwardly unattractive male parts?

As this transformation took place over many generations, the memory of having all of the necessary organs to procreate and all of the skills to be self sustaining went from a vivid memory to a historical recollection to a memory passed down in the subconscious ancient memory. Eventually when the smart ones all lost their unused penises, and the dumb ones lost their vaginas, an inexplicable feeling of incompleteness overcame them. This circumstance caused a deep subconscious awareness in each of them. They were missing a part of their being and were no longer a whole person; this forced them to seek out each other to fulfill the "half now you're whole" philosophy immortalized in song by Barbara Streisand.

For the Creationists, the first two young ones who were born in this condition of not having all of their equipment were a surprise to all of the others. Coincidentally born at the same time, they were also shunned for being different, as is still the practice; they naturally ended up pairing with each other. Since they were shunned, they decided to live elsewhere. You guessed it! They were Adam and Eve, and the place they moved to was a real nice new subdivision called, what else, Paradise. When Adam and Eve's offspring, Cain and Abel, came along, a couple of more odd ones were born to the other group. These two odd ones, who happened to be missing their male parts, were sent also to Paradise and began dating the boys. From this came the rudimentary beginnings of modern society. Modern society moved forward and developed into what we had when one of the boys killed the other one out of greed and avarice.

◀ THE BIG BOOK OF DAN

As the whole thing started to really percolate, and members of the tribal society became more efficient in their roles, a strange phenomenon emerged. As the dumb ones became proficient at the food gathering process, their counterparts, the smart ones, began to realize their dependence on the dumb ones for their very existence. They had given up these skills, trusting that they would always maintain their dominance over the dumb ones through intellect. As this scenario unfolded, it left the smart ones in a very vulnerable position. As the pendulum swung toward control of the group based on the ability of the dumb ones to gather goods and possessions, the smart ones tried to maintain control through various subversive activities. Denial of the hide-the-penis activity was a favorite ploy as the dumb ones had really begun to relish this activity and would do almost anything to be able to hide their penises. This was rather unsuccessful because the basic instinct of survival was alive in all of the smart ones, and consolidation of effort was impossible. There was always one willing to submit in order to get the necessities of living. This of course caused great stress to the community, and trouble ensued.

In an effort to quell upheaval, the smart ones enlisted the help of the dumb ones (who were not getting their fair share of 'Hide the Penis') to bring about social order. Rules were initiated to stop the sharing of goods to obtain favors. Another rule bonded one dumb one to one smart one for a period of time determined by the smart one. Disregard of the bonding rule carried with it a major penalty for transgressions by the dumb one. The penalty was the loss of those privileges and possessions previously gathered while hiding the penis with the smart one to whom the dumb one had agreed to be assigned. As the oldest profession was established in trading gathered goods for Hide the Penis, the second oldest profession was established to quell the problems it caused. This points to the legal profession as the second oldest profession, following closely behind prostitution. It was logical that in order to have a society, rules were needed to govern the group, and a specific person was needed to look after the adherence to those rules.

Well, somewhere in this chapter, I stated that the evolution of mankind in this manner is the only explanation for the way we are today, and I do believe this is true. It is the only explanation that fits. The activities we constantly participate in can only be explained as sub-subconscious thoughts that have their roots in some place and time with which we cannot identify. Some primeval force spurs us on to rationalize a totally unsupported, illogical lifestyle that has no basis in appropriate social growth.

In looking at what is commonly referred to as sex in humankind and mating in the animal world, it is nothing more than a means of procreating the species. It is a physical act urged on by the need to populate the world with like kind. In the animal world, it is assumed that mating has no other function than to procreate. In the context of humankind, the purpose of sexual contact is twofold; procreation is certainly one part, but a whole new social significance was at some time adopted. Why? Why should copulation take on the air of something other than what it was meant for?

This attitude must lie in some unconscious desire having no relevance to its original intended purpose. This desire has been passed down through the ages. It survives social stigma, stringent penalty, and even fear for one's own existence. It has brought kings to their knees, it has brought men of God to utter ruin, and it has spread disease, caused wars, and made numerous seemingly good marriages fail. Why? What the hell could there be about copulation with another human being that could be so fascinating as to create these seemingly hopeless situations?

Could it be that we are trying to replace the equipment given up so long ago and are in a constant search for the matching set of genitalia we lost in a previous existence? Could it be that we are trying to fulfill a secret desire to be whole again, not wanting to be half of anything? Could it be that, being driven by this unconscious desire, seemingly normal people turn into idiots?

Paradoxically, what about those who choose what is commonly referred to as the alternate lifestyle? They certainly are not looking to replace their missing genitalia. They are dating someone with like equipment. In observing these people, I have noticed that they typically portray social roles that assimilate a partner of the opposite sex to a degree that would suggest overcompensation for the lack of the customary organs. It is as though they like the *characteristics* of the opposite sex, just not the equipment. This would lead one to believe that gay men do not actually like other men; they just prefer their woman to have penises, and lesbian women don't like other women; they just prefer their men to have vaginas.

Oh well. It was just a thought while driving from here to there, an insignificant mental exercise, some time to kill. Never mind.

A follow-up note: I was watching the Doctor Oz show a couple of weeks ago. In this segment he was instructing women on locating their G spot. Toward the end of the explanation of location he made mention of the fact that the G spot was actually the remnants of the prostate gland left over from many years of evolution.

Ego

Ego has not served me well,
it causes my head to swell.
It makes me act perspicacious,
when perhaps I'm not sagacious
but instead in ignorance dwell.

A contrivance for self to deceive,
to state unequivocally what I believe.
To discount another's thought,
when in self importance caught,
to no other's ideas do I cleave.

Ego makes me pugnacious,
for validation I become rapacious.
Seeking kudos in a growing spire,
in a feverish frenzy, higher.
My value must have a real basis.

Should I feel self importance grow,
it's off to the library I'll go.
Perusing stacks and stacks,
all those well-worn books in racks,
I fathom how little I know.

People Who Need People?

No matter what our achievements might be, we think well of ourselves only in rare moments. We need people to bear witness against our inner judge, who keeps book on our shortcomings and transgressions. We need people to convince us that we are not as bad as we think we are.

Eric Hoffer (1902-83), U.S. philosopher.
Reflections on the Human Condition, aph. 144 (1973).

HUMANS ARE CONFLICTED creatures. These conflicts emanate from man's struggle to survive, which is generally in conflict with the natural order of the universe and with other humans' struggles for survival. Our need to form societies and rules to govern those societies causes those who do not fit in to these establishments to lead a conflicted existence.

For the maintenance of social order, a very basic rule was established. This rule dictates the coupling of two individuals for most of their existence. This coupling is called marriage. I am not sure of its origin. Man has always operated on the "more is better" philosophy. Those who were attractive to others probably had no trouble attracting mates. Those who had problems probably got together and conceived this rule to affect an even distribution of mates. Humankind set itself against the natural order in expecting that we could ever be satisfied with just one of anything.

Once marriage became an accepted social tradition, it became attractive to everyone who wanted to join or remain in the society. It has been strenuously encouraged ever since. It is considered an admirable condition by those who have never experienced it, an acceptable situation by those in it, and the scourge of humanity by those who have experienced it in their past but are no longer married. Ironically, while invented to reduce conflict and maintain social order, this practice of coupling has caused considerable conflict and social disorder.

The title of this story is borrowed from a popular song; the punctuation has been changed to protect the innocent. One line in this familiar song is a statement that tries to quantify the importance of the coupling of two people. "Once you were half, now you're whole" has been a misconception propagated for a long time. This concept completely breaks arithmetical rules and sets up an immediate mental conflict. As previously stated, it is a concept in complete opposition to the most basic rule of humankind, the "MORE IS BETTER RULE." This rule tells us that if one is good, then two are better, and so on.

The connotation of being only half of a person eliminates even a chance of survival unless you are coupled to someone else. This conflict encourages us to bond when our fear of survival is at its zenith. When you see your chance of surviving is actually being threatened by that "dumb son of a bitch" across the breakfast table who has not worked since the day after the wedding, you realize how this institution was falsely found on a premise vastly different from reality.

Survival is an individual activity only complicated by the addition of others who are too inept to do it on their own. Those who would have not made it through the culling process of the species on their own are always the greatest proponents of marriage.

If the notion of marriage followed the strictest form of linear thinking, it would have a greater chance of being accepted as a lasting concept. "Singularly you are whole, but by forming a symbiotic relationship with another hard-working individual, you will double your chances of survival." This provides a rationale for the union and gives each person a reason for continuing the bond. It would no longer be lyrical nor the stuff of which popular songs are made. To defend this viewpoint, I offer the cases of three individuals to demonstrate a typical, modern scenario of this half/whole theory:

PEOPLE WHO NEED PEOPLE?

The less-spoken-of side of our family included a particular branch attracted to living the life of carnival people. As you may have observed, carnival people have taken on a less-than- desirable air as judged by mainstream society and have a reputation as modern-day gypsies.

One couple, distant relatives of a cousin named Spot and twice removed, is chronicled only in the deepest recesses of family lore. The necessity of disclosing their existence, to point out the futility of life, outweighs my concerns for being ostracized at the next family reunion. Jocco and May joined the carnival shortly after their marriage. The wedding was the most memorable event of May's fourteen years on earth. It was quite handy to marry on her fourteenth birthday, being cousins and all; the whole family could gather and make it a combination wedding reception, birthday party, and family reunion. Seeing them exchange presents offered a touching sight. They gave each other gifts they both felt were symbols of their undying love: tattoos. Everyone stood teary-eyed as they stripped to the waist, each taking a turn in the chair, getting their names emblazoned on each other's arm, symbols of their everlasting union. It was unfortunate that the wedding reception turned into such a drunken brawl, as family reunions often do, but lucky for Jocco he lost only his bad front tooth – it needed a-pullin' anyway.

To get on with the story, Jocco's dream of obtaining a career as a highly paid truck driver shattered when the local truck-driving academy closed. There was some confusion over government funding for GI's, and the owner had to move suddenly to another country, somewhere in South America. As luck would have it, however, the carnival had come to town two days after the wedding. Jocco, with all the figuring he could muster, realized this could be his golden opportunity. Carnivals have trucks. They need drivers for those trucks. This would be his way out. He didn't mind the fact that he would probably have to start out at the bottom and work his way up; truck driving was worth the effort. He would study diligently, learn how to read road signs, use CB language, wear and accessorize trucker fashions – all of the necessary skills of a first-class professional. It would be hard, but with May's help, he believed he could do it. Thus Jocco's dream led them to the carnival life.

When Jocco and May made the big announcement to the family, everyone was excited to hear the news. Jocco would have a career, something no one else in the family ever had. The family was thrilled to help the newlyweds. They decided to give Jocco and May a new home to help them get started. Well, it wasn't exactly new, but the tires were almost new. It was Uncle Billy Ray's old place, and no one wanted it because Billy Ray expired in it on a hunting trip while skinning a coon in the kitchen. No one discovered him and that coon until three weeks later. Uncle Billy and that coon left a powerful remembrance of their passing. Anyway, with new home in tow, windows open, and curtains flapping in the wind, May and her new husband were off to find Jocco's dream.

Jocco worked his way up the carnival ladder of success. He shot from popcorn vendor up to chief mechanic in only two years. He felt he was on the verge of the breakthrough he wanted so desperately: truck driver. All he had worked for came close to materializing, but fate was not going to let it happen.

On the eve of their second wedding anniversary, Jocco and May were off to find a tattoo parlor to have second anniversary presents etched into their skin. They both looked forward with great anticipation to this custom. Their anticipation was perhaps their downfall. They stopped at the first parlor they found, a rather seedy place, but they couldn't wait any longer or go any farther. They had strong emotions for each other. They decided these personal expressions of the joy and rapture found in each other's company were not appropriate for viewing by the public. Expression should be viewable only when sharing naked splendor, where only they could see the majesty of the artist's work.

Two weeks after their second anniversary trip to the tattoo parlor, Jocco's tattoo became inflamed. Although at first the inflammation did not seem too serious, it turned into a chronic skin condition. It was so painful he could not sit for more than fifteen minutes at a time. This dashed all hopes of realizing his vision of taking May and the big rig down the highway to their dream home in the most beautiful trailer park imaginable.

Undaunted by this calamity, they set out on a new plan for the future. Because of his infirm condition, Jocco and May's dreams of wealth were forced to take a different direction. Putting their heads together, they came up with a new strategy. Jocco and May did not have the ability to gather wealth themselves because of the unfortunate tattoo parlor incident. Their skills in other areas lacking, they decide to invest in their most bountiful attribute, having babies. As each of the children grew old enough, he or she could work to help gather the family fortune. Who knew, maybe a truck driver would be in the passel somewhere! They decided to have as many kids as possible. Because each child would have a limited earning potential, the more children, the better the ability to gather riches. To stay on track, they would give the children names that represented their goal.

May began spitting out children at a rapid rate: first Diamond, a precious little girl, then Jewel, ten months later. After their third, Ruby Sapphire, Jocco became concerned that all he and May seemed able to produce were girls. He longed to have that son who could fulfill his truck-driving dream. Finally, on the fourth attempt, their efforts paid off. May gave birth to Silver, two weeks ahead of schedule and ironically in the chair of a tattoo parlor during their now ritual anniversary gift exchange. Although other children would follow, Jocco felt he had struck gold in Silver, his first male offspring. Jocco could not wait to buy Silver his first toy truck to whet Silver's appetite for those big rigs he would drive some day.

It wasn't until four years later on the regular carny circuit, while visiting their favorite tattoo parlor, that May realized Silver didn't seem to be growing much. She compared little Silver's height with the height of the tattooist's chair. On closer inspection, she determined he had not grown past the skull tattooed on her thigh the year before to mark his height at that time. They had decided to use tattoos as a

THE BIG BOOK OF DAN

record of the children's growth, rather than just as commemorative decoration. Because of the transient lifestyle, living accommodations often changed, and the standard mark on the doorjamb was not a possibility. (They had given up their trailer to Uncle Billy Ray's illegitimate daughter as part of her inheritance. This occurred after her mother saved up enough money for the DNA testing.) This whole episode sent May into quite a state. She knew how Jocco wanted Silver to be tall enough to reach the pedals on the big rigs to begin his training early. Jocco was certain to be upset.

Jocco upset was not a pretty sight at all. When Jocco became agitated, his skin condition flared up, and the worse the upset, the worse the flare-up. Shortly after the KING passed away, it was especially bad, and his whole behind turned bright red from scratching where it itched. With so many tattoos and that big red butt, from across the dimly-lit bedroom he looked like a baboon. Not an attractive sight when you're trying to bring your eighth little treasure into the world.

Well anyway, to try to keep the problem from Jocco, she decided to have another skull put just a little higher in a bare spot she found on her other thigh, in hopes that he wouldn't remember which was which. For weeks she wore Jocco's favorite dress, the one with the jagged hem line, backwards so the long part covered the original tattoo and the low slung back, which was now in the front, distracted him to the point of complete confusion. Literally saving Jocco's butt made it worth the stares of the other carny people. Besides that, she got a rush from all the people admiring the coiled snake tattoos around each breast, marking how Diamond and Jewel were almost as tall as their mama.

The scheme was working fairly well, but May knew it had to end soon. The dress had a mustard and relish stain from when a drunken customer in Wichita Falls insisted on feeding the snakes his hot dog. Although the relish had fallen off a week ago, the mustard was crusty. Besides that, wearing it to bed for the last month and sleeping next

PEOPLE WHO NEED PEOPLE?

to Jocco had given it a pungent odor. It would not be long before she would have to remove the dress to reveal the truth.

May did not realize how soon that actually would be.

The Carny arrived in Peoria on the first day of a two-day engagement. Silver hung out with Jocco out at the Ferris wheel, trying to figure out how to get the two screaming people down from the top after the drive quit running. Because of the sweltering heat, Jocco wore his powder blue Bruce Jenner jogging shorts. When looking down for his all-purpose trusty wrench (which he bought through a TV ad during the off-season), he noticed Silver's head still had not grown past the drops of blood tattooed below "MAY" on his leg just after the birth of the twins, Dollar and Bill. Just when those people at the top of the Ferris wheel needed him most, he became preoccupied over the growth rate of poor little Silver. Jocco's affliction acted up immediately, and the search for the savior wrench ended. He began to scratch and dig at his butt with all the fury he could muster, ripping and tearing at his Bruce Jenner jogging pants, howling and moaning as if the KING had been found, only to die again.

Word spread through the carnival. May knew the truth had slipped out despite her pains-taking efforts to save her beloved from the horrible truth. Jocco had found out Silver was not growing as fast as he should. Something was terribly wrong. May knew that for months to come she would be rubbing Gold Bond on Jocco's inflamed cheeks, trying to soothe his affliction. His pain would persist no matter how many stories about Elvis sightings she carried back from the grocery store tabloid rack.

The horrible truth emerged. Silver was a little person. He would never be able to fulfill his dad's dream of pushing the pedals, shifting the gears, and bringing home the big bucks that his birthing intended. He probably would not even grow large enough to have a reasonably-sized portrait of the Last Supper tattooed on his back. Jocco felt, to say the least, cheated and disenchanted that such a purely-led life in pursuit of the American dream could be dealt such a crushing blow.

In an effort to console her poor husband after months of torment and scratching (not to mention being thrown out of every men's dressing room in every Kmart from Peoria to Pascagoula), May decided on a course of action that eventually would prove to be their undoing.

One day, unbeknownst to Jocco, May went into a tattoo parlor in Cincinnati. She picked out a three-quarter bust of Elvis and had it etched on her inner thigh, just below her panty line, where it stared reverently up at the fountain of their perceived wealth. When completed, she liked it so much that she had the mirror image done directly across from it. She did this to surprise Jocco. She then had the opportunity to have that special dress cleaned during a prolonged engagement. She took it to a one-hour Martinizing place close to the fair grounds. May wore the dress until just the right moment arrived to present her special gift to Jocco.

Soon that special night came. Although feeling bad about the Silver situation, Jocco could no longer contain his lust for the beautiful and colorful vision of sweet, naked May. As they lay there in tattooed splendor, preparing to make a last-chance effort for wealth, Jocco peered quizzically at May's crotch. In horror, he reared back, gasping for air, scratching at his butt with intense fury. May drew back, screaming, "What's wrong?!" What's wrong?!" Jocco announced with utmost disdain that the tattoes looked like a set of google-eyed twins staring at Willy Nelson. After what the IRS had done to poor Willy, Jocco didn't have the heart to add insult to injury. From that day forward, the treasure trove remained untouched by Jocco.

While this was certainly an unfortunate incident in May and Jocco's life, the story does not end here in regard to Silver's development as an integral part of bringing the family wealth and happiness. It is, in fact, the beginning of the real story. Jocco finally admitted, because of Silver's diminutive stature, that trucking would not be the ideal job for him. Jocco had to focus his attention on training Silver for a job that would bring money to the family. Jocco was good friends with the Carny stilt-walker and knew the stilt-walker would be retiring just about the time Silver would come of working age. Jocco

PEOPLE WHO NEED PEOPLE?

decided stilt-walking would be a good career for Silver, and George the stilt-walker was willing to train Silver in the art.

Silver entered his apprenticeship with a modest pair of two-foot stilts that George had put away years earlier for just such an occasion. Because of the family's need for Silver to bring in money as soon as possible, Jocco forced him to keep the stilts on all day. He was allowed to remove them only at bedtime. What started out as a marvelous experience for Silver soon turned into a tragic situation. The stilts, being old, had no flexible joints, and this forced Silver to walk as though he had a load in his pants. Ironically, this also caused him to emulate Jocco's walk when Jocco had a flare-up.

Silver desperately wanted to fit in with the other children, but they excluded him from any activities because of his strange gait. These developments forced Silver to devote his childhood to becoming the best stilt-walker he could be. The lack of playmates and his father's insistence added to his frustration, but through all of this Silver persisted. Eventually, practice paid off. Silver's ability far surpassed that of his mentor. He became the premier stilt-walker in the carnival, his fame spreading far and wide. He made TV appearances and had an endorsement contract with a stilt manufacturer, all of which led to a more-than-modest income for Silver. With all of the childhood conflicts with his father, and Jocco's insistence that he wear those stilts constantly, Silver was anxious to leave his family behind. Breaking family ties became imperative, and this was the perfect time.

It was during one of his television appearances that Silver met the love of his life, Clydette, and her mother Betty Ray. Clydette, pushed along by her mother's dreams of fame and fortune, aspired to be a country western singer. During this same period, Silver became overindulgent in his desire for food and alcoholic beverages. He grew larger in girth, and weight began to hamper his stilt-walking. He maintained his presence in the stilt-walking world but dieted continuously and checked into clinic after clinic in an attempt to suppress his alcoholic tendencies.

Silver felt a very strong attraction for Clydette. During the courtship, he transferred all of his obsessive behaviors into one obsession: Clydette. The romance of Silver and Clydette was legendary despite the fact that he reached only four feet two and she, standing straight, attained a full six feet four. The height difference, however, did cause some self-consciousness in Silver. To combat this whenever they were in public, he wore a pair of stilts that made him a full inch taller than she. This situation kept Silver in a pair of stilts for the better part of every day, causing great stress to his legs.

When Silver met Clydette, her mother actively promoted her career as much as Jocco had pushed Silver into being a stilt-walker. Perhaps the sympathy Silver felt for Clydette's plight formed the basis for his original attraction, or perhaps his knowledge that her career was doomed from the start attracted him to her. Clydette had a rare and incurable condition that made her unattractive to the general public. Clydette had been born with a condition in which her brain developed inside out and backwards. From birth, everything that Clydette did was inside out and backwards. When she first learned to walk, she walked on her hands, backwards. Clydette's mother became obsessed with making her daughter a star, ignoring all the facts that were stacked against her. Clydette represented Betty Ray's only asset, and she had to try. Her tenacity was the only thing in their favor. Through tenacious persistence, Betty Ray taught Clydette how to do almost everything the normal way, except for playing her guitar.

Clydette could only play the guitar behind her back with her feet. The posture that she had to assume reminded one of a pretzel, kind of all twisted in on itself. In this position, her singing voice became rather shrill and lost the desired country western twang. In addition to this, she could only be presented to an audience by being hung from a special harness attached around her upper chest, which further hampered her singing. Betty Ray tried, but she secretly knew that if Clydette and Silver's romance failed, she would be without income.

Silver and Clydette's wedding was a gala affair twice as grand as Silver's parents' wedding. It was even larger than the wedding of his sister, Ruby Sapphire, to the carnival's owner. Silver's attraction to Clydette remained so strong he didn't even mind the pushy mother-in-law he was about to inherit. He did find out, however, through the duplication of their guest lists, that Clydette was actually the illegitimate daughter of Uncle Billy Ray and Betty Ray. This fact helped explain the strong attraction he had for her. After all, she was family. It also explained why he felt so at home in the house Betty Ray towed when he and Clydette first met. Jocco and May had started out in that same home.

After the wedding, Betty Ray still tried to push her daughter's career, but this activity took second place to ensuring that her new son-in-law kept working as much as possible. After six months, she gave up completely on Clydette and concentrated all her efforts on making sure Silver took every stilt-walking job she could dig up for him.

Clydette realized her career had hit the dumpster. She resigned herself to the fact that she was a failure and began a quest for self-improvement. Mom never stressed anything but music and singing; as in Silver's case, Clydette could not read, write or do simple math problems. This became her new goal. She pressed even harder toward this goal than toward success in her musical career. All this left Silver as the only one bringing in money not only for himself and his bride, but also for her shrewish mother.

Before long, disenchantment set in. Silver became increasingly frustrated with the situation, and he began to drink heavily and consume larger and larger quantities of food. He grew rapidly as these habits began to take over his daily life, but he continued to work. The once-famous somersaults became harder and harder for him. The stilts pressed on the bottoms of his feet. Every landing grew increasingly painful. Betty Ray pushed on and on, booking more and more engagements, to finance the purchase of more video learning courses for Clydette. Silver was truly living a far worse life than the one imposed on him by his dad. There seemed no escape for him. Where would it all end?

◄ THE BIG BOOK OF DAN

Then one day, the inevitable happened. While putting on his socks, Silver noticed the sagging and wrinkled skin around his ankles. Although he may have noticed this before, he had apparently ignored it, denying it was happening to him. Now he couldn't ignore it any longer. It was too bad to deny. He had to see a doctor to confirm it, but he felt sure he had it – the dreaded disease of an over-the-hill stilt-walker.

Secretly, Silver made an appointment to see a specialist, the same doctor who diagnosed George, sending him into early retirement. The doctor poked and prodded at the masses of wrinkled, rumpled skin on Silver's legs. He took X-rays, measured, and poked some more. The diagnosis was as dreaded as Silver had suspected; the visit only confirmed what Silver had already known. From years and years of walking on those stilts, his overweight condition, and flipping over and over landing on his legs, the bones were degenerating and getting shorter while gravity pulled the skin down, rumpling it up around his ankles in large, purplish folds. The disease that would end his life as the premier stilt-walker of the century was upon him. He had the dreaded, horrifying condition that all stilt-walkers fear. He had rumpled stilt skin.

His retirement party proceeded predictably, with hand shaking, clichés, and fun for all, but it also left a predictable emptiness in Silver. It was over for him. The only life he knew, the only source of income he had to support Clydette and Betty Ray, had been taken from him. He walked dejectedly out of the tent that night, never to hear the cheers again. As he pushed open the flap and walked into the night air, he felt absolutely alone.

The first two days after Silver's retirement flew by quickly. The phone rang continuously with condolence calls from friends and relatives. On the third day, the phone didn't ring as much; by day four it quit altogether. His life savings dwindled rapidly. The bills were piling up with every visit of the mailman. Between Clydette's education video tapes and Betty Ray's hot line to the home-shopping network,

◄ 46

PEOPLE WHO NEED PEOPLE?

Silver sank deep into debt. He had nightmares of the big rig pulling up to his home, connecting the tow ball, and pulling his residence away as he stood and watched. It was living hell for Silver as Clydette and her mother just lay there in the living room, dialing "800" numbers and ordering this and that as fast as they could. His back against the wall, he had no choice. He had to do it.

Silver pleaded no contest to the charge of attempted armed robbery of the 7-Eleven at the corner of his street. They had all the evidence they needed. His face didn't appear in the video; only his hand, holding the revolver, stretched up over the counter into the camera's range. His voice came across only indistinctly as he shouted, "This is a stick-up!" into the candy rack. But there was no denying it. As he hobbled out of the store in the powder blue Bruce Jenner jogging shorts that were his inheritance from his dad, the video camera captured the evidence, proof positive for all to see: rumpled stilt skin.

The law sentenced Silver to three to five years in a minimum-security prison, and he soon was packed off to serve his time. The prison being overcrowded, Silver was billeted in a nice trailer while the new building underwent construction. It felt very homey to him. His worries over supporting Clydette and Betty Ray eased when Clydette landed a job reading Literacy Council notices to the illiterate, and Betty Ray became a regular on the afternoon talk show circuit, bouncing from one show to the next, claiming to be whatever they were looking for.

Clydette visited Silver regularly the first two years he spent in the joint. She looked forward to the weekly conjugal visits. As they sat on the edge of the bed, conjugating verb after verb in the room provided for these types of visits, she could not help but wonder why a more classroom-like atmosphere wasn't provided. After two years of visiting Silver faithfully, she stopped coming to see him without ever explaining why.

The real reason she stopped visiting resulted from a misunderstanding she had when discussing prison conditions with one of the guards. The guard related to her that Silver had gotten scrod at dinnertime every Friday, so far, during his two years in prison. Clydette became furious when she found this out and left the prison, never to return. She had been faithful to Silver every single day of those two years and had never once gotten scrod by anyone. Her last video tape on verb conjugation pointed out her error: scrod was not the past perfect tense of the word screwed, but by then it was too late.

The authorities released Silver from prison after he completed the third year of his sentence. He did not leave as the broken man you might expect. After a life of trying to please other people, Silver was finally the way he came into this world: alone. He realized that in trying to please others, he had not allowed time for the things that pleased him. He never wanted to be a truck driver. He never wanted to be a stilt-walker. He wanted to be an orthodontist. His dream had always been to be a traveling orthodontist, going from town to town, carnival to carnival, in a modest Winnebago, putting braces on the teeth of all of those unfortunate carny children. It would be a long road, but he would make it, and he'd live a rich and rewarding life.

While having fun portraying relationships, I have tried not to stereotype males and females. With the current changing of gender roles, it is no longer possible to portray "typical" roles. Gender is often interchangeable in today's society, and, at least in the United States, people are victims of the external forces of parental, peer and societal pressures.

While watching the news, watching your neighbor, or watching your own family, you have to ask yourself, is our society, with all of its status pressure and performance pressure, working? Are we missing the real meaning of life? People are not doing a very good job of solving the problems of society on any level. The nightly news is a nightmare, divorce rates are soaring, and violence is escalating worldwide at a horrifying rate. All of these phenomena can be proven with statistics, calculations, and body counts. All the linear devices we invented to add up our successes are, in fact, tolling our failures.

PEOPLE WHO NEED PEOPLE?

To the student of history or anyone with a good memory, it may be noted that man's plan for man has never changed. Since the beginning of recorded time, the motivation of man – to survive – is like a Xerox copy, reissued repeatedly. Perhaps it is time to put something different in the Xerox machine, to redefine the notion of need. Dependence on others for our personal gain is not working. Being part of a whole, a subdivision of the whole, is not providing what we need. Being part of a pyramidal, organizational chart where someone always stands on someone else's shoulders mandates that greed and avarice be part of the daily existence of man. Providing the need for power only motivates people to seek power. Perhaps the wholeness we seek from others is not the answer. Perhaps the wholeness we seek is simply inside us. Maybe there is something grander just within our grasp.

Footnote

SOME COUNTRIES STILL maintain a more traditional line when it comes to role playing or fulfilling other's expectations. In certain countries, people are born into professions that are carried on for generations. Being born into these professions in traditional roles is accepted and even appreciated because life-long careers are hard to come by. These carry-overs from ancient kingdoms have places and positions for everyone.

I would like to present an interesting example of this "traditional role." Sultans are revered as the leaders of their countries with no other qualification than being born. Their countrymen wholly accepted this. Because of a sultan's position, he was not expected to provide for his people. Instead, they were expected to provide for his every physical need and desire. They fed, bathed, dressed, and moved him from place to place and even assisted in his intimate bathroom habits. In order to ensure protection of the lineage, this last-mentioned duty fell to one of the sultan's most trusted servants. This esteemed position even carried a title commensurate with its importance: Sultan Pecker Shaker.

The Narcissist

I regret it right off and know I will pay,
when I ask my neighbor, How are you today?

I'm doing great, let me fill you in.
Don't you think that I look really thin?
I'm going out to a luncheon date,
I'm already at least a half hour late.

I'm going on vacation to Napa Valley.
Jim's building a pergola out back in the alley.
I do wish he and the kids could go,
but these days it's so expensive, you know.

After lunch, it's a bikini wax.
then pick up six pairs of slacks at Saks.
After that, it's Chico's for three new skirts,
then Walmart to get the kids some shirts.

At 3:00 PM, it's my anal bleaching,
then a self-awareness class Joyce is teaching.
Dinner at 6:00, in the microwave,
To cooking, I'll never be a slave.

At 7:00 I hurry to Cole Hahn
to try six new pairs of shoes on.
Then Victoria's Secret for thongs and bras
(no shabby undies seen at the spas!).

Finally back home, I'll flop into bed,
while Jim's busy making me fresh breakfast bread.
We've decided not to have sex anymore –
I recently told Jim it's just such a chore.

Next time I see you, I'll have a new car!
Please, remind me to ask how you are.

I Survived! Or Did I?

Self: All I can tell you with certainty is that I, for one, have no self, and that I am unwilling or unable to perpetrate upon myself the joke of a self. . . . What I have instead is a variety of impersonations I can do, and not only of myself – a troupe of players that I have internalized, a permanent company of actors that I can call upon when a self is required. . . . I am a theater and nothing more than a theater.

Philip Roth (b. 1933), U.S. novelist.

IN LOOKING BACK at my life, my parents and Catholic school were the most influential forces in forming my public "I." This was accomplished through mortal fear of reprisal by my father and some very fierce Nuns that I surely didn't want to anger.

Moving in silence, black and ominous, weapons hidden, not to be revealed until the attack became imminent the grim reapers of battle were waiting, watching, circling at a distance, radar on, ready to pick up any movement in the enemy camp. They stalked, looking for signs of weakness, ready to pounce at the first opportunity. Their battle garb had all of the trappings of the ancient warrior: the armor, the weaponry, the forbidding demeanor. Each could have taken up arms in any battle of old. They could have captured Gaul for Caesar, or decimated the Moors in the Christian crusades (which would have been more fitting of their station), or laid siege to the garrisons of Hannibal. Each time, they would have been the victors.

They were the foot soldiers of Catholicism. Ever dreaded, ever feared, angels of destruction, they were NUNS.

I stood as one of the opposing warriors in the great battles of Saint Ignatius in the time between 1954 AD and 1962 AD, when the wars were fought in skirmishes over the winter months between October and May. These months were chosen strategically. An annual October meeting occurred between the Lord and Lady of our serfdoms. During this time, the Crusaders allied themselves and assured these mercenaries of Christ that we were rebels in our own lands, and any punishment meted out would be applauded. It was generally accepted practice among us rebels that being in as good a grace as possible helped to disguise our true intentions: not to be singled out too early so that in ensuing battles the culprits would not stand out. It was, after all, a rear guard action, an undercover assault based on surprise, rather than a full frontal attack.

One cannot explain Catholic school to anyone who attended Public school. One had to *live* the experience, and those who did could relate only to others who also lived it. A knowing grin could be detected on compatriots when you uttered, "I went to Catholic school," and nothing further needed to be said. Even today, the nuance the horror is lost on children attending Catholic school; since the reformation, it is just not the same. Involved at the peak of approved corporal punishment and inhumane practices, I remember savage times when the conflicts, at their zenith, reached a fevered pitch. Back then, Nuns indiscriminately implemented all forms of warfare to conquer us, the enemy. Psychological, chemical, and outright physical punishments brought us to our knees. Trial by the sword was common place. Should I, at any time in the future, be captured and tortured by any other army of aggression, I would not be intimidated or have fear in my heart, for I could rise up in their midst and say, "I WENT TO CATHOLIC SCHOOL" and render them powerless against me. They would know I had faced the worst many times and survived.

I SURVIVED! OR DID I?

I began my career as a foot soldier, as most did, amid the rabble of kindergarten. This is the time you are most susceptible to the onslaught of outside forces. We had very few recruits later on in the upper classes. My indoctrination as a Catholic school kid was very attractive to my parents, tuition hadn't been thought up back then. The experience was free: discipline, motivation by guilt, religious training, and education rolled into one, all free. What parent would, or could, pass up such a deal? For sure, not mine.

Although I had a brief stint of one semester in public school kindergarten, it was not to be my lot to continue there. Saint Ignatius opened up its curriculum to include kindergarten, with the likely intent of capturing the young and unsuspecting before they had a chance to develop any bad habits. When my Mom told me the news, I was petrified; I winced thinking of the terror that awaited me. My brothers told me daily of the inhuman treatment doled out. Without firsthand experience, I approached the legends of abysmal torture and excruciating punishment with a wary fear but yet with a degree skepticism. The first painful crack of ruler's edge across my young tender knuckles reinforced all of the storied fables whispered in the halls of Catholicism. However, with no recourse offered, it was off to Catholic school for me at the tender age of five years.

I stayed on the outskirts of danger rather than directly in the battle like some of the less seasoned troublemakers. Although almost caught several times, I had learned well from my two older brothers what I could afford to do and what I should not chance at any cost.

Despite this, I, along with one other compatriot, Jimmy Neusbaum, carried on covert actions under the noses of the Nuns in such a way that capture remained almost impossible. We had vastly different styles, but the outcomes were similar. My style of taking on an angelic air resulted in any suspicion soon being rescinded. It worked well for me. Jimmy, however, had a completely different ploy that worked even better than mine.

Jimmy had coal black eyes and long, straight, thick hair; I can still see him vividly in my imagination, although I have not seen him since the fifth grade when his parents moved him away. Jimmy had one unforgettable feature, or maybe a combination of features, that remains with me. In reflecting on this, it must have been his complete demeanor that was so impressive. Jimmy had a gawky way about him that made everyone assume he had not enough intelligence to get in trouble, nor the ambition. I think this impression came about primarily through his stare.

There are two types of stares confronting educators. There is the glimmer-of-hope stare. This is the one you see most often. It is the one that lures you. Your first response is that the person peering out from behind this blank look is too dumb to live, but every once in a while, you recognize comprehension. This fleeting impression gives you the instant desire to fill that potential with everything possible before it recedes again into the void. This stare produces an overabundance of attention rather than a lack of it. The recipient can't help himself from doing all he can to aid the person behind this particular gaze.

This glimmer-of-hope stare was not Jimmy's. Jimmy developed the stare of utter hopelessness. The one that is so blank that it is viewed as virtually impenetrable. The one that makes you believe that if you even look at it for a moment, it will actually suck all the knowledge from you into a vast abyss of nothingness. It was a marvelous tactic on his part. Not only would the Nuns not pay attention to him, they actually would go out of their way to avoid looking at him, so far out of their way that if you sat one seat away from him in any direction, you were sheltered from their attentions by the umbrella. This, coupled with my angelic appearance, allowed for a complete school year free from suffering the corporal wrath of Christ's crusaders. The great professors of the "turn the other cheek" (so I can get a better shot at you) philosophy.

Jimmy and I had no friendship outside of school. I can't remember ever seeing him anywhere other than rounding the corner of the driveway that led into the school lot each morning and inside the school itself. I have no idea what the rest of his life entailed or how successful he was at it. But in the arena of learning, he excelled. The most memorable event of the year, the climax to previous events, was timed so perfectly it will always remain as *the* memory of my fifth year of schooling. Jimmy had spent much of the year staring blankly at the goings on, quietly twirling a drill bit between his thumb and index finger, patiently drilling holes in his history book, math book or whatever book we were supposed to be studying. As the trees budded lime green and our sap was rising, his books were so full of holes they were unreadable, and he now had a hard time finding a spot big enough for the drill bit to bite into. Jimmy had finally lost interest in twirling the bit into his studies and needed something else to occupy his attention while Sister Mary Terrance droned on.

This new something, not yet revealed, would turn into the ultimate coupe and mark Jimmy as *strategist extraordinaire*, although it also became the reason Jimmy's parents decided to move away, never to return him to St. Ignatius.

As a means of torture, we were ordered to use a certain type of pen. An old-fashioned ink pen, the type that used liquid ink. Ink you could not erase or write over, ink which caused the rewriting of many a paper because of a misspelling or a stray mark just words from completion. A hated device, this pen was reviled by all its users. The particular one we were instructed to use had a nib end and a barrel that unscrewed, to allow you to drop in an ink cartridge without squirting the girl next to you.

On this particular day, Jimmy had bored his last hole into a textbook and sat gazing into space, both hands still for the first time all year. Momentarily lost, he almost let that unwanted glimmer creep into his eyes, but suddenly he was drawn back: an idea had hatched. He slowly unscrewed the pen and removed the cartridge, set the barrel and the cartridge down on his desk, and inserted the nib end of the pen up his nose, grasping the nib with and the screw thread up. Slowly he began twisting, twisting, and twisting. The nib end slowly worked up into his nostril, mining deeper as he twisted. He turned it until only the nib protruded, barely pinched between his thumb and finger. He then proceeded to try the removal process by reversing direction. He had gone a turn too far.

For the first and only time in the school year, Jimmy raised his hand. The momentary thrill of this fled from Sister Mary Terrance when she realized it was not a gesture of participation, but a cry for help. Upon close inspection first by her and then by the school nurse, they decided to send Jimmy to St. John's Hospital for the extraction.

Jimmy returned to school late in the day with a wad of cotton protruding from his nostril held in by a strip of white tape wrapped around a red swollen tortured nose. Jimmy's usual seat no longer open to him. He was assigned a seat just within reach of the left hand of Sister Mary Terrance, within ruler distance, to prevent any future episodes. Luckily, the school year was almost over. That was the last year for the immortal Jimmy Neusbaum, but his memory lives on. He probably got lucky and went to public school.

Catholic school and my parents were the most influential forces in forming my public "I." The mortal fear of reprisal for not living to expectation and feelings of anxiety over not being accepted by others kept that public image striving to please.

Never being conscious of private self versus public image during those years, I lacked awareness that they even existed. I thought it natural to act in a manner to please those around me when needed but to think as I would in private. I spent many years acting out scenes as I thought I was supposed to in an effort to survive in the "we-ness" of social situations.

In situations where "we" is necessary, the "I" is relegated to the back seat in an effort to make "we" work. The private "i" is easy to miss because that is the "i" that is in service when you are alone. It has no function in the "we" situation and therefore is not presented for judgment or comparison in the presence of others. Most are unaware of it and think there is no difference between their public and private selves. The distinction remains unapparent unless it is pointed out to you by someone to whom it has been previously pointed out to. Even under those conditions, most people do not believe it's a reality.

I became aware of "i" in a seminar on how to become a better sales person. It was a revelation of great importance to me because for many years my wife said I had a chameleon-like personality, changing as needed to suit the situation. For many years I could not understand her accusation. Although "I" had no idea what the hell she was talking about, I was willing to do whatever it took to do what she wanted. After all, my public self acted to discover whatever would elicit her approval. It is as true as true can be that there is a public person and a private person in all of us. The public person has been nurtured for years by all the outside influences to get it to perform in the "we" situations such as dating, marriage, work, school – all of those places where you need to be a "we". The private person is rarely so well looked after.

Not being aware of this situation is a confusing matter in itself, but not being aware of it in social circumstances makes them unbearable. I spent many years in conflict with myself, both persons wanting equal time. But the inner me always set itself aside for the outer me so that I could be part of a "we." What a confusing mess to live through, but "I" made it through and "I" found "i" and eventually learned to give him equal time at the sacrifice of the "we." Yes, I have survived, but for many unfortunate people this is a deep mystery and paradoxical in its existence. In effect, we are paradox personified; trying to find the "we" outside of us blinds us to the fact that there is an "i" going on inside of us.

The reconciliation of "I" and "i" and admitting to their mutual existence begins to turn many things from one perspective to another entirely. Once this understanding is achieved, the motivation of "I" is understood and the interaction of "I" with "i" makes a "we" true to the self. The superficial interaction of the internal "i" with the external "I" becomes less demanding. "I" survives and "i" emerges, making a "we" who is less dependent on outside "we's," and making all of the outside "we's" less desperately desired and therefore easier to come by. It is a paradoxical fact of life that no one wants to form a "we" with another who seems desperate. "We's" are only attractive if they contain enough strength to service "I." Wow! What a tangled morass of mixed-up shit the linear world presents to us.

Integrity

It's been sold for gold.
It's been sold for a penny.
Once it's sold, you don't have any.

The Consolidated "I"

Awareness: The man who is aware of himself is henceforward independent; and he is never bored, and life is only too short, and he is steeped through and through with a profound yet temperate happiness. He alone lives, while other people, slaves of ceremony, let life slip past them in a kind of dream.

>Virginia Woolf (1882-1941), British novelist.

AFTER RUNNING YOU around a couple of times in the last chapter, "I" thought it might be good to offer some other thoughts on the "I" – its dangers as well as its rewards – but first I want to relate a poignant story on a "we" situation that I experienced in the not-too-distant past. This experience caused me to do some research in the areas relating to the experience, so I will start with disclosing my research information and then move on to the actual event.

The area of research in which I became involved had to do with the wandering tribes of the world: their customs, traditions, and methods of entertainment. One noteworthy fact is, because they are wandering people and the areas they wander in seldom have roads, their means of conveyance is usually something other than a car. There are basically two types of wandering tribes, those from the Middle East and those from the Far East (which are both linear terms that I am not too sure of because I don't know where East stops and West starts). Although the Middle Eastern tribes and the Far Eastern peoples both roam as they please, the reasons and motivations for their wanderings are very different.

The Middle East is a barren, desolate area of the world. This area has long been a desert with only abbreviated areas of greenery, called

THE BIG BOOK OF DAN

oases. The tribes would go from oasis to oasis to barter and trade necessary provisions with other tribes. The traditional routes they followed were based on the seasonal direction of the winds.

The Middle Eastern tribes travel in the direction in which the wind blows in order to keep the moving sand at their backs, out of their faces. Because they travel in such a manner, seemingly powered by the wind, they have become known as the Pneumatic tribes of the Middle East. This is reasonable; I can understand why they are so named.

The Far Eastern peoples are of a mysterious nature in their travelings, not seeming to have a motivation or direction behind spreading across the lands of Europe and Africa. After much research into their wanderings, I found no concrete evidence that there was a pattern to their travels. With no explanation found, I can only assume that their motivation was perhaps a religious one based on the dictates of their spiritual selves and outwardly manifested in their clothing. As the Middle Eastern tribes were Pneumatic, you might say that these people were turban powered.

Anyway, the entire quest to find out more about the peoples of the Eastern tribes was inspired by a music concert that I attended recently. A concert like this one could only be described as moving. A once-in-a-lifetime experience, it left me with a tear in my eye and a burning desire to understand more about the origins of this music and the traditions of its practitioners. The constant meandering of the Middle Eastern desert tribes and the harsh environment in which they live gave birth to this musical tradition.

The desert is a dry environment, as explained to us by those wonderful guys on the 'ology shows. In this environment, the customary musical instrument does not fare well; reeds dry out, wooden instrument dry and break, and valves on brass instruments become stuck and unusable. With the constant travel from oasis to oasis, it would be very difficult to maintain these types of instruments. Since the mode of transport, the camel, had certain weight restraints, it was impossible

THE CONSOLIDATED "I"

to carry unusable belongings on these endless migrations. The people needed a form of entertainment more suitable to their lifestyle. As these tribes are ageless, and no formal libraries kept the information that I obtained by hearsay and am about to disclose, hopefully this information is not some fictitious bit of hot air.

This musical art form began during the early Egyptian period. It was born from the wish for entertainment to pass the long evenings, and it has been passed on ever since. This music is held so dear to the practitioners that an annual competition determines the best musical groups, and these are the ones that go on tour every year. I witnessed this same age-old form of musical entertainment at the aforementioned concert, so what I heard that unforgettable night was the best of the best.

The music was performed by a group of four, similar to a barbershop quartet, each having his own part and, in consort, playing a harmony. The music was produced by controlling the sphincter muscles in such a way that, as gas passed through the restricted openings, musical notes resulted. Because of the quantity of gas needed, there were no solo parts but instead a continuous, four-part harmony. It struck me that this was the epitome of a codependent "we," analogous to the mental image of the bicycle built for two.

Because of the media used to produce the music, rigorous dietary training is part of the musicians' regimen. Finding the proper opening sizes of sound boxes in a combination of four individuals makes it difficult to put together an award-winning group. Bass is the hardest position to fill, and this group imported their bass from a Turkish prison.

I must tell you that their rendition of "Amazing Grace" caused a stir in the audience that I have not witnessed at any concert before or since. It was quite rewarding to watch the group perform, and they richly deserved their name. No one who attended will ever forget the *Toot-in- Commons* but, because there was no solo star, as individuals they will probably remain unknown.

Oh, by the way, I have tickets for two front-row seats to see an up-and-coming group called the Sphinxters if you are interested.

This brings us to a discussion of the consolidated "I" versus the forever outside "we," and the natural stages that are passed through on the way to the consolidated "I." Out of necessity, the first stage of life is the dependent stage. It is the stage that sets the tone for early life.

Sometime just after your birth, a new sensation arose. This sensation was something never before felt: hunger. It was an irritable sensation, but you did not know what to do about it, so you did the only thing that you were capable of doing – you cried. The effect of your crying brought about a result. Someone fed you. At that moment in time, you learned you could cause a change in the behavior of those around you by crying. You could translate all of those irritations into a whimper, a cry, or a bellow depending on how bad the irritation. Someone would try his or her best to satisfy your needs if for no other reason than to shut you up. This was the start of many years of whimpering, crying, and bellowing about all of those things that you wanted others to do for you. As the years went by, you learned the finer arts of whining and manipulating. Whining and manipulating are not effective strategies until you are mobile enough to follow your victim around.

During the years when you had no choice but to depend on others, consistent rewards for manipulative behavior convinced you it was very acceptable. The fact that others did the same thing in similar social situations made it feel normal, and therefore there was no reason to change this behavior. As you grew older and were able to provide services to others, they began whining at you. This was the phase change from a dependent person to a codependent person.

This phase of existence lasts for many years. For people who have great, perceived needs and little means of fulfilling them, it may never end. There is, however, a risk involved in this codependent stage. Just as you depend on others for your needs, they also depend on you for theirs. This codependency causes a constant bartering situation

THE CONSOLIDATED "I"

to occur. For most people, when the time spent fulfilling the needs of others consumes more time than is spent enjoying those things they have obtained by whining, the situation becomes unacceptable. This is the point in life when you become willing to forgo many things just to enjoy the things you already have. You begin to realize that most of the things that you thought you needed are really not needed at all. There are some things that you will never be able to provide for yourself, so you have to depend on others for them. Those items become fewer, however, so you do not have to barter away as much time as before. At this fuzzy juncture of the next phase, you are becoming somewhat of an *inter*dependent person, but for the most part an independent person.

The independent phase of life is full of pitfalls. It is the time when most people who decide to exercise this independence find themselves in divorce court. The independent person begins a period of alienation from children, spouse, siblings and parents. All of these relationships were born during the dependent or codependent stage and now are viewed as burdens to the independent person. Job changes eliminate the codependent work relationships developed in the past dependent stages. The myriad problems encountered at this time cause many to run back shrieking to the codependent phase, but, for those hardy few who persevere, the rewards are there. This is the juncture when you realize that you are responsible for yourself. This is the time when you begin to act upon the world rather than expecting the world to act upon you, and you stop acting out a persona just for public acceptance. This is the time when those opinions that bound you to things you did not believe in no longer matter to you, and when your opinions no longer bind others to you, and you do not feel betrayed by them. This is the time when you realize that life is a singular journey, when the precious few years you have on the earth become a joyful experience and you begin to know yourself. You stop whining and crying about what you want from others and get it for yourself. You become a consolidated "I."

It is hard to find people today who are willing to advance to individuality in our society. Looking back in history, it is much easier to find examples of individuals who fit this category of the consolidated "I," or what many would call individualists. Teddy Roosevelt, Harry Truman, certainly were standards for the celebrated individualist. These were those who were willing to be responsible for themselves and live their lives as they wished. It is an oddity of our society that they are revered and celebrated and yet not emulated. More and more, we choose to be part of groups, tribes, committees, and teams so that we can avoid being responsible. We choose to hide in the crowd and go along with the group. It is now fashionable to blame everyone but ourselves for every predicament in which we find ourselves. *It's our parents' fault, it's the school's fault, it's society's fault* we whine, in order to not face the fact that, if we are not individually responsible, then no one is responsible. The consolidated "I's" are still out there but have chosen to live their lives without the approval of the masses.

They are easy to spot if you know what to look for.

The consolidated "I's" are those who no longer hide their inner selves for fear of what others may think of them. The fear of other people's opinions is for much of our lives a governing force. This fear of offending others and not "fitting in" influences how we dress and act, squelches joy and happiness, and makes us prisoners in our own bodies. No one asks for this power over you; it is automatically granted due to years of conditioning regarding the importance of belonging. This fear of other people's opinions weighs heavily on us. It is hard to dispel because of the fear of what they might think of us if we don't *care* what they think of us. The absolute worst part of this situation is that we cannot control what other people think of us. We may be doing all the things that we feel will gain the approval of others only to find out that, although they outwardly seem to approve, their inner feelings are quite different. However, they can't express those feelings for fear of *your* opinion of *them*. We live our lives, or at least some part of our lives, trying to give people the right impression.

THE CONSOLIDATED "I"

We perform based on our perception of how others see us, only to realize that they are so engrossed in garnering the favorable opinion of others that they will never tell you what they actually think of you. They are too afraid of what you may think of them, and so the game goes on.

Another device society has foisted upon us is the fear of failure. The fear of failure is closely linked to the fear of the opinions of others. The need to succeed is part of living in a social situation. If society rewarded failure, there soon would be no society. Someone has to make the whole thing work, so we have set up a system that judges success based on linear score keeping and bestows great honor on those we decide are winners in all phases of activity. This reward system places someone at the top, someone at the bottom, and everyone else somewhere in between. This system is heavily weighted to give most of the reward to the person at the top, perhaps a stipend to the second place finisher, and an honorable mention to third place. This system encourages those few who have the necessary physical and mental performance attributes to participate. Those who do not have these attributes, and therefore have no chance to succeed, are relegated to spectator status. The reward system was, at some time in our past, probably set up to find the most desirable candidate to propagate the species. This same behavior is seen in animals; it is the process of natural selection, but at some point in time it became perverted by custom rather than carried out from necessity.

The linear concept of rewarding skill levels gives way to judgment of ability, and rather than hold ourselves up to public ridicule, we will choose not to try rather than to fail. This fear of failure holds many would-be greats at bay and narrows the field of competitors. The consolidated "I" gives up the fantasy of ever being great at things and learns that the pleasure of doing is reward enough for the effort. The consolidated "I" is quite comfortable with the realization that the joy is in the doing, and the doing is more important than the trophy. The consolidated "I" knows that "I can't" is really a contraction for "I won't because I may fail."

The members of the *Toot-in- Commons* found reward in being part of a group. Many people find it rewarding to be part of a group. The group receives recognition for collaborative achievements, but seldom is recognition given individually to its members. Many acknowledged group members sink into oblivion and feel inadequate once no longer associated with the group. Those members of the group that stand out as leaders, are recognized, and as such are remembered as individuals, deflect the possibility of failure. The great part of being the leader is that your personal fear of failure can be eliminated by dispersing this failure among all the members of the group. I think that being a group leader does not necessarily qualify one to be recognized as a consolidated "I" because reward is still the goal of the leader. Being the leader is just a clever way around taking responsibility for self but still gaining the reward. The true consolidated "I" does not need reward as a motivational tool. The true consolidated "I" places importance on doing for the joy of doing but is often rewarded inadvertently. Most people recognized posthumously as great had the courage to play their own music even if it sounded remarkably like a fart to everyone else.

After the independent phase has gone on for a while, it becomes a lonely place and most people then begin to gravitate back to some social situation for contact with other people. At this phase, the consolidated "I" begins to seek out people with similar interests. This is a wonderful phase of life and is well worth the wait. You no longer feel the need to give in order to get. No longer are you encumbered by all the necessary commitments of the dependent phases nor do you feel the need to exercise independence when you want interaction with others. You get to pick and choose what you want out of the life you were given. Be extra careful when you enter this phase because there are some out there that covet it and think they can live vicariously through you. They are still in the codependent stage and will try desperately to drag you into their dilemmas.

Nose Hairs

They grow at an alarming rate,
pop out whenever you're on a date.
An inconvenient fact of life,
like taxes or your ex-wife.
You clip them at the nostril rim,
or pull them if you're Jungle Jim.
At checkout, the cashier will stare.
Did a rogue hair pop out of there?
They're straight, thick and raven black,
never curly, grayed or slack.

Taxes we might alleviate.
Your ex-wife might accept a date.
Nose hairs, we could cultivate
(maybe Guinness would measure and rate).
A neck wrap for cold weather,
in hurricanes, a convenient tether.
We could dye, bead and braid 'em,
or just sit there and hate 'em.
Whatever you think, they're here to stay,
like taxes, ex-wife, and ex-fiancée.

Berm Bingo

Introduction – The Game: How It Came About

THE PURPOSE OF this book is fun. In offering a little fun and a little philosophy for the traveler, the hope is that all those hours you spend having your life dominated by the person holding the key to the car (which is also often the key to your bladder) will not keep you from having all of the sport. Yes, they have the joy of cussing at other drivers, outwitting the radar gun, deciding where to stop for the night, and the privilege of being key master, but you get the consolation prize. You can exercise your powers of perception in a little game and force them to compete on a less-than-equal footing. A convincing score, along with a well-placed bet, could give you the freedom often reserved for the master of the keys.

Chapter 1: The Roundabout Origins of Berm Bingo

BERM BINGO, THE game, is the outcome of an active mind traversing a monotonously flat expanse of country. A stretch of land where watching the corn get taller is the only scenic treat available to the traveler of the four-lane highway, a stretch of land where everything blends into everything else, where everyone blends into everyone else. Specifically, this was a monotonous stretch of northern Indiana where I lived for sixteen years.

I don't wish to seem critical, and having been reared in Cleveland, Ohio, certainly does not give one license to criticize the rest of the country. Being a Browns fan and a follower of the Indians, which I am (or was) does not lead one to believe that I actually have a mind at all. Having to live down the fact that 'the river that runs through it' caught fire about the same time the Mayor's hair did does not leave much room to knock one's surroundings. Coming from the biggest little city in the Midwest and living through the period when the mere mention of your roots brought scoffs and outright laughter from most everyone still did not prepare me for the culture shock that is Indiana.

Most people who lived outside of Cleveland would not find Ohio and Indiana to be so different. Both are Midwestern states with farming as a major part of their economies, but Cleveland was an island of cosmopolitan in a sea of rural. It held a flavor of many cultures, a blending of rich ethnic flavors not found in the white-bread society outside of the city. It lacked the lackluster quality of everything that surrounded it. There you could hear the neighbors argue in Russian and smell industry percolating up the street, mixed, when the wind blew from the north, with the aroma of Lake Erie. (When I lived there, I always knew where north was; since moving, I have lost my sense of north). I've never found that feeling of vitality in the sprawling landscape of rural America.

Reared on the near west side of Cleveland, my neighborhood was like those of most other big cities. Houses, as I remember them, squatted on large lots set back from the street by an expansive front yard, and the sidewalks leading up to the front porches seemed almost endless, especially when it was snow-shoveling time. Spindled railings enclosed porches. Those railings had almost the same effect as the glass that surrounds a car passenger. What happened within the confines of those railings was magically invisible from the street and allowed the porch sitter to view the world outside without fear of involvement or reprisal. At least that was my impression of what people thought, based on what went on behind those railings. My father often tested the limits of the theory by sitting on the porch in ill-fitting boxer shorts on those long, hot summer evenings. The boxers with the fly that spreads open when sitting and never quite closes when you stand. The railing concept, although seemingly a common belief, was one I did not share. I knew it to be untrue based on the "GREAT WHISKEY BOTTLE INCIDENT" of 1954.

The "GREAT WHISKEY BOTTLE INCIDENT" occurred during a particularly hot summer day in '54. I was five. My older brothers had no interest in playing with me, for reasons I do not wish to go into. My father was at work, my mother busy with housework. It was rubbish day. Back then, we had rubbish day and garbage day, probably a carry-over from the Second World War when the country did recycling (not a new idea at all). All of those things that were not garbage, such as cans, bottles, and old lamps, were set out in designated containers, awaiting the trash collectors.

In 1954, you had to make your own fun: not much on TV, not an overabundance of toys, and no playgrounds in our neighborhood. As I looked for something to do, I walked by the rubbish containers, and a beautiful bottle caught my eye. Oddly shaped, the sunlight danced off its multi-faceted exterior. I captured this magnificent prize and moved on. As I passed another house, I found another bottle. It was the best thing ever to a boy of five, house after house, bottle after bottle and no one around to take them from me. These treasures were all mine, a wealth of beautiful bottles out there for the taking. I went home, got the American Flyer, our family "sport and utility" vehicle, and began to collect those marvelous bottles. By mid-morning, I had an assortment of bottles that anyone would envy, all lined up, one after the other, on the front porch for all to see. The trash men had come and gone, so I had all I was going to get, but I had enough – a porch full of bottles of all shapes and sizes, with hardly a repeat in the bunch.

I swelled with pride over my bottle coup – until lunchtime – when Ma emerged from the basement in her usual housedress, hair tousled, to see what I had done. She walked out on the porch. She gasped. A look of absolute horror came over her. She was as mortified as the time my brother repeated Dad's favorite word in front of Aunt Magdalene. Her look and posture gave me the instant sensation that I had done something wrong, but what? Who wouldn't appreciate such glorious workmanship? She sure didn't! Clearly, she did not covet this fine assortment of empty whiskey bottles as much as I did. In a wild frenzy, she gathered them up and packed them off to the garage.

Over the next year or so, she doled them out, two at a time, to the rubbish can. She carefully buried them among tomato cans, ketchup bottles, and other refuse to prevent rumors that our family could have emptied all those bottles.

This near-tragic incident alerted me to the fact that the railing was not a mystical barrier. Ma knew this to be true, I knew it to be true, but who else knew the truth? Certainly Pop didn't know or he would have taken the time to put some pants on. Certainly Peggy, the girl across the street, didn't know, or she wouldn't have done what she and her dates did on her porch. Judging by the actions of most of the neighbors, Ma and I were the only ones who knew, and I would never tell.

My brothers, a sadistic pair, used any incident to torture me, however slight. They would have a field day with the whiskey bottle episode. Once, they took my dad's tire chains and some tent pegs and staked me to the front yard for the better part of a morning. They left me there while they went to play baseball. Ma, doing housework, didn't know what they had done. I lay there until she heard me yelling for help.

Getting back to my memories of houses in the neighborhood, I realize what I recalled as true was not always so. Upon recently revisiting the old neighborhood, I observed that it had strangely shrunk in all dimensions. The front yard barely allowed enough space from curb to porch to squeeze the lawn mower through. The distance from our front porch to the opposing front porches certainly gave the ladies across the street, at least those with reasonable eyesight, a good idea of the magnitude of my dad's equipment. The rambling mansion I remembered actually resembles a two-story shoebox. My memories were from the perspective of a five-year-old boy, which seemed real, until I toured the neighborhood as a much older boy.

Although raised in this intimate tribal society called a neighborhood, eventually my time came to strike out on my own exploration of the world. As I grew, the CAR enhanced the range of my wanderings. At first, I begged rides by thumb extension. As my friends and I grew and were able to reach the pedals, we would walk to other neighborhoods to borrow cars from people we didn't know. More importantly, they didn't know us, or, should I say, could not identify us. Eventually I got my first car and further increased my traveling. Soon the big city became available to explore. I achieved citizenship of the entire city, not just the neighborhood, and the sounds, smells, attitudes, and ethnic flavor all became part of my culture. I was a big-city guy.

Now rest assured, I have not forgotten the focus of my meandering. I am making my way to how Berm Bingo developed, and believe me when I say that my minor digressions are necessary to inform you of the significance and universal nature of the game.

Once secured, a car becomes part of your nature, an extension of you for the rest of your life. It enhances your ability to search for all of the other perceived necessities in an ever-expanding area. One of the necessities of an eighteen-year-old male, as it remains today, was sex, not just hit or miss dating-type petting, but situations that had regularity and frequency and full frontal nudity. Possession of a car provided a lure. The better the car, the more alluring. Male birds use color to attract mates; other animals use their physical prowess. We guys used cars. We are the only animals on the earth that do not employ natural selection as a means to breed a healthy species. We resort to other bait to attract the opposite sex. The search becomes ever more maddening when what we think is a sure-fired way of getting laid turns out to be not as sure-fired as expected. Regular sex still eluded me. Eventually I found a flawless plan for taking care of sexual desires. This is an age-old strategy devised, I think, by women. I got married.

Along with getting married, I got the product of sex on a regular basis: responsibility. The responsibility of a wife, children, a house payment, all of the things that are connected to getting laid whenever you want, which is also a myth. This ever-increasing spiral of responsibility eventually led to seeking more money. The need for more money eventually led to moving out of Cleveland to secure a better job and a better life for my newly organized tribe, my family.

The migration of my wife, children, and me occurred with the promise of fame and fortune as a District Sales Manager for a company in Chicago. Because all the arrangements were made in Chicago, the big city seemed to be part of the deal. The interview took place in Chicago, the agreement to work for them was made in Chicago, but I never saw where I would be located until the deal had been made and notice given. By the time it hit home, it was too late; I would manage sales in Fort Wayne, Indiana. I went from urban to rural in one big flop! I could almost feel the manure oozing between my toes as I walked into the motel on that first night. I went from having a vague idea of meat processing to knowing the pet name of the pig served for dinner. As I lay in bed on that first night, I felt fear creeping into me, not of a new job or the move to a new way of life, but fear of my wife. She, too, had been reared in Cleveland, and even more than I, she was BIG CITY all the way.

In the ensuing months, between my initial move to Fort Wayne and my family's arrival, I tried desperately to cushion the blow for my wife. During this time, she stayed in Cleveland completing all those things associated with relocating. The house was up for sale, the movers had been contracted, the groundwork was being set down, and all systems were go. She had not yet been to Fort Wayne.

I did not realize her concept of Indiana until the day she started talking to real estate agents about her new surroundings. To this point, I had felt relatively safe in assuming that she had no idea of the size of the city or its cultural leanings. Or how different it was from Cleveland. In my view, safety lay in her ignorance. How wrong I was. By my intentional lack of information, I actually hatched in her an opinion totally opposite of the one I hoped she would have. This became evident when the real estate agent informed me of one of her questions.

"Do you have libraries in Fort Wayne?" she asked. His response was, "Yes we built one right after we ran the Indians off." I never heard from him again.

In the three months that I lived in Fort Wayne while she prepared to move, I lived in a Red Roof Inn, occupying myself with learning the business by day and acquainting myself with the local culture by night. My wife only visited on one weekend trip to pick out a house. The duration of her visit and the amount that needed accomplishing did not leave much time to look around. When she returned to Cleveland, her new surroundings were still a mystery to her. Either that or she entered a state of total denial. I was not sure, but whichever, it left some time for my acclimation to the new environs and allowed my feelings of bliss to continue.

Over the next three months, the house sold, our son Adam's school year ended and all was readied for the move. We became a family, all under one roof again, in September of 1979. With all the activity of moving in and arranging our new life, things had yet to settle into a routine. I remained unscathed and personally reinforced in my belief that my wife had accepted the move wholeheartedly. I inhabited a fool's paradise. Soon the full effect of the move would hit.

We had grown particularly fond of a brand of cheese corn, not nationally distributed but found in only one store we knew of in our neighborhood back in Cleveland. In the confusion of packing and making ready for our departure, my wife forgot to lay in a supply sufficient to last until we could go home for a holiday or funeral. Shortly after landing in our new house, and nearly unpacked, she realized the depletion of cheese corn was imminent. Over dinner that evening she made the announcement; the cheese corn needed to be restocked, and she was Cleveland bound. In a vain attempt at appeasement, I offered pork rinds as a local substitute, going so far as to ensure her that pork rind technology had advanced to the degree that bristles seldom appeared in them anymore. This all to no avail, and at the first opportunity, we were off to Cleveland for cheese corn.

You may still wonder what this has to do with BERM BINGO, and assuredly, I am coming to the point in the very near future.

What I had taken for acceptance actually existed as denial, a denial so strong that to this day if asked, "What city are you from?" her natural response would be Cleveland. Although in truth, I am not sure of her response because we don't travel together since the divorce. I would be willing to place a small wager on her answer, though.

The promise of financial fortune was the only solution I could think of to appease my wife and to ease the difficult situation I had created for myself. So off I went to find my fortune.

My only choice seemed to be the life of a traveling salesman. I accepted my lot with relish; after all, the price of cheese corn had increased three hundred fold, including the cost of gas, food for my wife and children en route, trinkets for the natives, and of course the cheese corn itself. Consequently, I formulated my plan, found customers, made appointments, and learned my trade. The only drawback to my plan resided in a small item of information I had neglected to tell my new employer. I had never actually sold anything before.

Only those who have never done it covet life on the road, and I proved to be a prime example. Nights full of all the steak and seafood that a stomach could hold and all the party time one desired, without the hindrance of someone keeping track of your comings and goings – it would be great! It was going to be the greatest time one man could have and still get a paycheck. Although I had traveled in previous jobs, trips had always been of short duration. My new travel arrangement boasted an unlimited expense account, no one to answer to except the road ahead, and only a bit of an undefined quota to worry about. As unaware of the rigors of this life as my wife was of life in Indiana, I would soon receive a full dose. Meanwhile, I eagerly anticipated embarking on the good life. After all, at an early age I had read, "On the Road," the great Kerouac account of road life, and I felt ready for adventure. What lay ahead certainly did not contain what I had imagined.

"On the Road" from a salesman's perspective is no bargain. The imagined good time ended with a resounding No from the first candidate I called on. The sting of rejection bit hard when he handed back my shiny new business card, refusing even to consider my services as necessary to him. This experience proffered my first taste of things to come. Less than pleased with this first attempt at selling, one word and a scowl abolished my dream of heaven on earth. A scowl worse than even those doled out for the most grievous infraction of etiquette from the nuns back in elementary school. I instantly came to a full realization of the rigors of my chosen career. By the end of the week, it became clear how much like work this was really going to be. Mile of highway to drive, rejections, bad meals and empty motel bars: paying for all those cheese corn runs back to Cleveland would not be easy. Although tempting, quitting did not enter my scheme, failure was not considered. After the first week, my future materialized as a bleak picture. Thursday night, driving home from the last call with nothing to show for my week, was difficult, but the solitude of the car, with no people chattering and no phone ringing, became and is to this day, my safe haven.

The inside of a car on the highway is a more effective place to think than even the bathroom. Other than rote memory skills required to guide it down the road, very little thought is necessary. You have hour after hour available for self-improvement, deep thought, planning, plotting, and as much observation as the mind can accommodate. The advantage of the situation balances the disadvantage of not being able to respond to many stimuli. This allows all the processing time without the need to take action. If you hatch an idea, the time to evaluate it is available. Observing something that looks interesting leaves an impression that it actually is interesting. The ever-changing view bolsters our quest for instant gratification and stimuli. For those pseudo-nature lovers, it offers the ability to get close without getting too close. For the food addict, it offers an ever-changing array of restaurants, refreshment stands, drive-ups, drive-throughs, drive-ins, or drive-arounds, any way you want it. Yes, the car out on the highway offers all you want! Or does it?

When rivers were the popular travel routes and boats the favored mode of transport, the banks that contained them sifted out and deposited debris. Along these banks, one could find anything that had been discarded, dropped, or washed in from some exotic place upstream. People spent hours walking along, looking for treasures to use or barter. Things of beauty, worth, or substance would bring feelings of luck and good fortune to the finder. The subconscious memory of the good feelings provided by treasure hunting on riverbanks provided the designers of the highway system reference for adding a similar feature to our modern highways. That little extra bit of pavement outside the solid white line, the berm, or soft shoulder, is analogous to the banks of a river. That trace of non-road, non-earth nothingness where you stop your highway yacht in periods of distress is where the flotsam jettisoned from the traveler is caught, strained out of the system, and remains until a modern scavenger picks it up. Unfortunately, the only item of bartering worth in today's marketplace is the aluminum can, so the rest lies there until the local prison inmates take their spring walk down the berm to remove unwanted refuse.

Finally, this is where BERM BINGO fits in! Passive activity usually occupies most of the time spent flying down the highway: thinking, talking, or thinking about talking. The exchange of conversation in such situations requires much thought because you should avoid volatile topics. It is best to reserve religion, politics, and like conversation for less confined spaces so as not to piss off your traveling companions. It's a bad time ahead for those, traveling across country, who have angered the key keeper someplace near Toledo with a noxious comment about organ size in the heat of battle over the policies of the current president.

BERM BINGO offers a game similar to the one you played in Dad's car when you were kids. Back then, it involved spotting certain makes of cars, but back then cars were distinctive and models limited. To play the car game now would require hours of study as well as a good pair of binoculars. There are so many makes and models, and to add to the difficulty, they all look much the same. The only way to determine one from another is by emblem or logo, and, unfortunately, those too are similar.

BERM BINGO, however, requires only a fair perception of a few animals in their live condition and a reasonable idea of which part of the country they are native to. The game does not deal with specific breeds or species, only general categories. You may play continuously, in spurts, or any way you like. Only in rare instances, such as spotting the remains of a white rhino in Kansas, do you receive the lifetime achievement award and become excluded from the amateur ranks. In this case, you are confined to playing with other fortunates, such as the guy that spotted a bull elephant along a stretch of I-10 just outside El Paso. By his own admission, it turned out to be only a large piece of gray canvas billowing in the wind, but because he went unchallenged, the sighting was scored as an elephant. In his conquest, this player excluded himself and is restricted from future play in the amateur ranks.

The general idea of BERM BINGO is to spot and identify the remains of the poor creatures that have been unfortunate enough to venture from their natural habitat onto the highway. Since they have not given their lives to a noble cause such as sport or feeding the hungry, it is a way of recognizing their passing as having value, be it ever so trivial.

(A side note: pointing out their demise reinforces the "LOOK BOTH WAYS" lesson for your children.)

Games need rules, so in the next chapter you will find rules and suggestions for playing BERM BINGO. You can play this game anywhere there is a road. I have provided rules for guidance that encompass many situations. If you should feel compelled to add special rules, such as LA freeway rules or desert rules, by all means do so. Please keep in mind that it is a game, like tennis, played with decorum. It should be played with a more friendly gusto than, say, kick boxing.

Chapter 2: Rules of the Game

THE GAME OF Berm Bingo is not for the squeamish. It's a game that broadens the players' horizons by making them aware of the animal world around them. This happens without having to hike up any mountains or through dank forests. It does not inconvenience the players by making them do any physical activity and does not cause

THE BIG BOOK OF DAN

discomfort by exposing them to the elements. The game is played from the comfort of your vehicle.

The object of the game, simply stated, identify objects laying by the side of the highway, and score points. The one with the most points at the end wins. Wins what? That's up to the players.

Berm Bingo in its purest form uses only dead animals as game pieces. Because of human expansion, some parts of the country are devoid of sufficient species to make the game interesting. Inanimate objects may be included or not, depending on your specific interests.

Berm Bingo could benefit mankind in many ways. With so many animals spotted daily, it could suffice as a means of checking animal populations. The automobile could serve as a mobile classroom for budding zoologists. By including inanimate, discarded objects, it could become a rolling anthropology study of our societal habits: what we eat, drink, and find valuable enough not to discard (conspicuous by absence) in the piles of junk ejected every day from our cars. The automobile could become a classroom for the advertising whizzes who market fast food. They could scrutinize the effectiveness of their packaging and promotional campaigns, getting a handle on market share just by observing the litter as they pass by. What a boon to humanity this little game could be!

As is the case with any game, rules are important, so rules we shall have. It is impossible to gauge cunning without some standards. It's also perilous to enter into any game without knowing the boundaries. I am providing rules in this chapter in a form that you may alter accordingly for your company and circumstances. Just keep in mind that everyone needs to agree on the final set of rules. What fun is cheating if there is no chance of being caught?

A) GENERAL RULES
1. All players must have a clear view through the windshield.
2. Dashboard or visor obstructions giving advantage to one player are prohibited.

BERM BINGO

3. All players must be awake and lucid during the game period.
4. No two-vehicle play via cell phones is allowed. I hate those f#*%ing cell phones.
5. All game pieces must be on the berm, entangled in, or resting on the guardrail. No out-of-bounds calls are valid.
6. No living creatures qualify. Vultures picking at a raccoon carcass are scored only as a raccoon.

B) **URBAN GAME VARIATIONS**
   1. Urban game variations only apply to boundaries of city limits. This distinction must be made by the driver in an audible tone and responded to by all players.
   2. In Urban situations, the boundaries are curb, or gutter, and the narrow strip of lawn between curb and sidewalk. The major portion of the game piece must lie within bounds for a valid call. Should challenges occur, measuring is certainly an option, but the game is halted during the challenge procedure if any player is absent from the vehicle.
   3. The dead rule is in effect at all times for game pieces. **Quality of life is subject to opinion and not considered in this game.**
   4. Point values for Urban games are scored only after **RULE B.1 is followed;** Rural rules are used in all other situations.

C) **RURAL GAME VARIATIONS**
   1. In traversing from Urban to Rural, the driver makes the distinction and all players must respond in an audible tone. Anyone not responding will be considered not fully conscious and disqualified.
   2. Should a game piece be spotted just past a city-limits sign while the vehicle is still within the city limits, Urban scoring is in effect. Should you decide to increase your score by waiting until the sign is passed, Rural scoring is used, even if Urban / Rural call is not made by the driver. This is a situation where timing and gamesmanship are crucial and add tension to the game.

D) URBAN / RURAL GAME VARIATIONS

1. In situations where frequent changes from Urban to Rural scorekeeping are too complicated, either Urban or Rural scores may be used if all agree. Otherwise, follow rules as stated.

E) REGIONAL VARIATIONS

1. Should you be traveling where berm is not a regular part of the Highway Department's budget, berm shall be defined by mutual agreement.
2. Common regional slang names are acceptable only if recognized by the indigenous peoples (i.e. polecat for skunk).

F) TERRAIN IMPEDIMENTS

1. Inability to sight down the berm due to large, jutting rocks, etc., shall be considered an impediment.
2. In such cases, all calls shall be made after the passenger's side door is even with the impediment.
3. In cases of winding roads, the apex of the bend shall be the forward limit of play.
4. When traveling uphill, the peak of the hill shall be the forward boundary.
5. When traveling downhill, the peak of the next hill is the forward boundary.
6. All impediments, such as oddly placed road signs, shall be treated as in rule **F.1.**

G) INDIGENOUS SPECIES

1. In reviewing the list of scoring values, it may be necessary to add species indigenous to your area. This is done by mutual agreement and can be based on historic records and past sightings.
2. During long trips in previously untraveled areas, indigenous species may not be known. In cases where a sighting is not

covered by the list, a point value of 1 will be awarded, unless it is clear that such an animal is not indigenous to the country in which you are traveling (see Chapter 3: Scoring).

Chapter 3: Scoring

IN CHAPTER 2 the rules of the game were outlined, defining how the game is played. Now it is time to quantify how well you play. It is important to measure the ability to perform an activity. By comparing oneself to others, proficiency is established. The ability to beat the next guy is increasingly important in our society. A resurgence in the popularity of many games is a recent phenomenon not only with the habitual competitor, the male, but also with the female. Keeping score has become the most important part of participation. Games, personal conquests, paychecks, number of vehicles, type of vehicles are all forms of scorekeeping. I have published a scoring system for you to use as is, or it may be used as a guide to creating your own value system, which many seem to be quite adept at.

Scoring can become a very passionate and heated endeavor. Due to the confined space of the gaming area and the close proximity of the players, it is important to have a common understanding of the point value of the game pieces before the game begins.

The thought of being stranded alone on the berm because of an argument over the value of a dead dog is not pleasant.

I have published the following point values for animals common to the mid-western and mid-southern areas of the country with the understanding that they may be less than relevant to other areas. This guideline is used as a basis for your scoring system, and may be added to or revised as necessary to reflect more accurately the area you are traveling in. For example, if you are in an area where it is common to see a dead farm animal along the highway, you may wish to devalue the farm animal, or if it is rare to see a dead raccoon, you may wish to increase this point value. The spotting of extremely rare or out of place creatures, such as an elephant in Wyoming or an ostrich in

◄ THE BIG BOOK OF DAN

Cleveland, should be instantly voted as a lifetime achievement, creating an instant winner.

Please keep in mind two very important concepts. First, the point value system should be understood by all before the game begins. All point value revisions, as well as added objects, must be so noted in writing as a reference for all. **Secondly and most importantly, the dead rule is always in effect.** The sighting of a live rhinoceros standing by the roadside brings you nothing in point value.

POINT VALUES

SPECIES	RURAL	URBAN
Raccoon	1	10
Opossum	1	10
Skunk	1	10
Deer	1	10
Cat	2	2
Dog	5	10
Woodchuck	5	20
Chipmunk	7	12
Muskrat	10	30
Snake	10	50
Turtle	10	50
Squirrel	30	1
Wolverine	15	35
Porcupine	15	35
Bird (non-flying)	20	30
Bird (flying)	30	40
Common farm animals	5	50
Bear	100	150
People	100	5

POINT VALUES

DEBRIS	RURAL	URBAN
CLOTHING		
One glove	1	1
Pair of gloves	50	50
One shoe	1	1
Pair of shoes	50	50
Hat	1	1
Sunglasses	1	1
Shirts or blouses	1	1
Pants or skirts	5	1
Dresses	6	2
Men's underwear	10	1
Ladies' underwear	1	10
Scarf	10	10
Coat	10	20
Wallet or purse (empty)	5	1
Wallet or purse (contents)	5	100
FURNITURE		
In poor condition	10	1
In good condition	100	100
CAR PARTS		
Muffler without tailpipe	1	1
Muffler with tailpipe	5	10
Muffler with tailpipe and engine	50	100
Parts unidentifiable	1	1
Parts identifiable by type	30	1
Parts identifiable by make and model	50	10
Pieces of tire tread	1	1

DEBRIS	RURAL	URBAN
MISCELLANEOUS		
Condoms	1	1
Cans (aluminum)	20	1
Cans (steel)	1	1
All debris not listed	1	1
ROAD ALLIGATORS (see Chapter 4)		
Male	50	50
Female	100	100

POINT VALUES (ODD LOTS AND ENDANGERED SPECIES)

1. **ODD LOTS:**

   Circumstances may be such that at times you see a group of animals of varying species clumped together in eternal repose. An example of this may be a dead vulture or raven within pecking distance of a rabbit. This is a rare sight, to which any traveler of the highway can attest. This rarity needs to be recognized and celebrated as such. In this scenario, the successful spotter is awarded the total of the individual scores with a multiplier of three. Please note that herd animals, such as deer or wildebeests, should only be scored by their book value and head count.

2. **ENDANGERED SPECIES:**

   Sightings of endangered species are extremely rare events for more than one reason. First, most people, including this author, cannot identify which species are endangered. Secondly, endangered species typically only inhabit areas we have not been able to traverse. If these areas were convenient to mankind, those endangered creatures would probably be way past endangered. In such instances where the astute naturalist can prove the species as endangered, the lifetime achievement award should be bestowed and that player eliminated from amateur play.

BERM BINGO ➤

DEDUCTIONS (MISIDENTIFICATIONS and CHALLENGES)

1. MISIDENTIFICATION:

The misidentification of game pieces is inevitable. A wrong call is going to cost you! If stringent penalties are not applied, the person making the call feels no compulsion about waiting to properly view the game piece, and thereby might employ the strategy of purposefully making wrong calls, preventing others from making proper identification based on closer observance. **To prevent this type of less-than- admirable play, point values will be deducted *double the score for the game piece called by the offender.***

If no challenge occurs, even in the case of an erroneous call, the player making the call shall be awarded the point value of the animal that he/she called (See *CHALLENGE PROCEDURE* below).

2. CHALLENGE PROCEDURE:

The challenge is as inevitable as the misidentification. The procedure is outlined here to set guidelines for challenges. The game piece in question must be challenged between the time the call is made and the time the game piece is even with the front bumper of the car. When a challenge is called, it is up to the challenger to correctly identify the game piece and give reasonable evidence to the correctness of this identification. When the call is an obvious misidentification by the original caller and all players agree, the points will be deducted from the original caller and points will be awarded to the challenger. Should no decision be imminent, the driver can stop the car at the option of the challenger or the original caller so either party may more closely inspect the game piece. This may be necessary in the case of turtle calls, in as much as it is hard to tell their status, and the **Dead Rule** is always in effect. If neither party makes an inspection, a third-party referee can be appointed to validate either player's call or award points. **The decision of the referee is final in this situation.**

◄ THE BIG BOOK OF DAN

- *NOTICE*: **CAUSING ADDITIONAL GAME PIECES** (once living creatures as opposed to inanimate objects) **TO BE PUT INTO PLAY IS A STRICT INFRACTION OF THE RULES. AN INFRACTION OF THIS NATURE WILL RESULT IN DISQUALIFICATION UNTIL THE VIOLATOR INSTIGATES THE REPLACEMENT OF THE GAME PIECE.**

DURATION OF PLAY (TIME-LIMITED, MILEAGE-LIMITED, and UNLIMITED)

1. **TIME-LIMITED GAMES:**

   The time-limited game is one way of playing. This allows all passengers the opportunity to participate for a period comfortable to them. The time-limited game can be any period that all players have decided on, but it must allow enough scoring opportunities to make the game interesting. In a state like Indiana, the trip from one city to the next provides ample chances for all players to rack up points.

   The official clock must be in view of all the players. Because of recent advancements in dashboard clocks, accuracy is assured. The set-up of this game is flexible enough for combo-games where you are using Urban /Rural rules. In these situations, the speed change vs. scenery opportunity ratio is variable, thus making the mileage game seemingly less competitive. By using a specified factor such as time, all players have something to work against while they are also working against each other, adding an extra bit of tension to the competition.

2. **MILEAGE-LIMITED GAMES:**

   This type of play is suited to long trips where speeds are constant and stops are few. If this game format is preferred by your traveling companions, it should be noted that the game continues for all periods of travel within the set mileage chosen. Should you spot a dead cat near the parking lot of the truck stop as you are parking to go eat, it is a valid call and credit should be allowed.

◄ 92

3. **UNLIMITED GAMES:**
The unlimited game is only for the tenacious. This game should be subscribed to by all players because it is similar to a poker game where once you fold, you're out. This means no sleep periods are allowed for the weary. Each player has the burden of witnessing all calls, giving a distinct advantage to the idiot you are traveling with who takes great pride in the ability to drive non-stop on every vacation trip. Be wary of the person suggesting this game. You may be doomed to stay fully conscious from Minneapolis to Miami.

Chapter 4: Road Alligators

A little learning is a dangerous thing;
Drink deep, or taste not the Pierian spring:
There shallow draughts intoxicate the brain,
And drinking largely sobers us again.

Alexander Pope (1688-1744)

IN THE SCORING section of the last chapter, reference is made to this chapter for an explanation of one particular animal, the road alligator. The road alligator is one animal of which many of you may not have heard. In this chapter, discussion of the road alligator will provide you with familiarity.

The road alligator is present and visible in so many places and so often; yet, it goes unnoticed and is virtually ignored by all but the very curious observer. Therefore, I felt it necessary to give the road alligator special attention. I hope this will raise the consciousness of the less-seasoned traveler and add to the enjoyment of those who currently find the road a less-than-exciting environment. It may enhance your ride if you are more knowledgeable about surroundings outside the scope of your immediate concern. This knowledge will give you a new appreciation of the world around you. I think some people could do with a new appreciation of their surroundings.

The road alligator (Alligator roadensis) is one of the strangest and least understood creatures in the world today. It has never been featured on Wild Kingdom, been portrayed in a Disney movie, or even politely mentioned in a zoology program. Although found in great numbers, it has never been considered an alternative food source for the world's starving population. Despite being hunted for its hide, it has never been protected by Greenpeace. It has not even been "much maligned" for any of its actions during capture.

Yes! The road alligator does exist. Not only does it exist, it flourishes when many species worldwide are waning in the throes of man's onslaught to claim all resources as his own. The road alligator is a creature of marvelous adaptive powers. It is cunning in its inconspicuousness. Careful to fit into a barren, desolate, and dangerous environment, the road alligator has become even more adept at survival then the revered cockroach. The road alligator lies out sunning itself, placidly daring the world to confront it, to try to take back the territory claimed from humans. The road alligator is a true master, thriving when many lie dead nearby. It has conquered mankind by becoming so inert that most deem it useless. Inertness has kept it out of the sights of rifles. Inertness has ensured it a life by rendering it non-threatening.

The unassuming nature of the road alligator and its inclusion in **Berm Bingo** makes it necessary to explain its existence. The ability to identify the road alligator will put it at risk, but when haven't animals been at risk when it comes to game and sport? This gives all gamesman an equal opportunity to recognize and identify this creature, making the game more exciting. Perhaps knowledge of the road alligator will enhance its chance for survival by making you mindful of it and more careful to ensure it no harm through careless driving habits. With this in mind, I will now tell you about the road alligator:

The road alligator (Alligator roadensis), more than likely a very distant relative to the American alligator (Alligator mississippiensis), has developed along a very different path than its reptilian cousins. The road alligator does not rely on streams and lakes for its habitat. Although at times it has been spotted in culverts, the road alligator does not depend on a watery environment. It has grown accustomed to all types of weather, none acting adversely on it. This adaptability has been of great benefit to the road alligator's ability to flourish in all areas of the country.

By its peculiar, well-developed, migratory habits, it has been able, over years of evolution, to shed its legs. Unlike other animals, it relies on man for transportation to its breeding grounds. Man's range of travel has been the only obstacle to the road alligator's expansion; it cannot migrate into areas not inhabited by humans. Unlike its relative the American alligator, which is confined to the temperate zone, the road alligator has extended its range beyond that. It is found in all parts of the United States and many foreign countries.

The mating habits, gestation period, and birthing information of the road alligator have not been widely studied; consequently, no definitive information is available. A breakthrough in this area seemed eminent when Jacques Cousteau announced plans to "film the mating 'abits of zees wonderful creature." Unfortunately, the project was canceled due to a lack of interest on the part of the French playing card industry. They refused the necessary monetary support. Concerns over an inability to sell the product of such an endeavor caused them to pull out early, before the climax was reached, which left poor Monsieur Cousteau gasping. Again, the road alligator thwarted man's intrusion into its world of inertia by simply doing nothing. Circumstantial evidence and logical conclusions based on the mating habits of other similar animals are all that can be used to surmise when, where, and how this species mates.

It is assumed that temperate climates are conducive to the mating of road alligators. The lack of sightings in colder regions during winter months leads naturalists to believe that these are migratory animals like geese, ducks, and butterflies. This is borne out by the fact that the road alligator may be seen by roadsides during all seasons in southern states. I observed countless pods of road alligators along highways in Florida during January and February while on weekend excursions with a female friend. The warm weather of springtime also brings many sightings of males and young alligators along roads in the northern states. Although the northern population of the road alligator is severely decimated by the snowplow, the creatures bounce back each spring to repopulate those regions.

The full-grown male has been noted in lengths up to 12 feet, but again, no official records have been registered. The female of the species is more elusive. The female can, however, be easily recognized by the white stripe along the side of its body. Its girth is smaller than the male's, and the female does not attain the male's length. The female is approximately 7 feet long when mature. Again, I stress, the female can only be distinguished from an adolescent male by its characteristic white stripe. This fact is important in **Berm Bingo** because of the scoring potential for spotting a female road alligator, and the potential loss of points for misidentifying an adolescent male as a female.

The only known predator of the road alligator is man. A number of road alligators are captured each year by prison road gangs. The reason for this is unknown. They do not create any product from the animal. The only logical explanation is that they do it for sport. No weapons are used in the capture. The thrill of grabbing a grown alligator and wrestling it into a sack or slinging it into the back of a truck must be what drives the convicts. Occasionally, employees of state highway departments will join in the hunt but with noticeably less enthusiasm. Highway department employees account for far fewer captures than do prison inmates.

The only other predatory action of any consequence is the capturing of the road alligator for the use of its hide in manufacturing soles for sandals. This activity is not widespread and is only conducted by a small group of craftsman. It consequently does not account for the loss of large numbers of road alligators.

The discovery of and information about road alligators is recent.

No anthropological evidence has been found linking them to ancient tribal rituals. No digs in the plains of equatorial Africa have, as of yet, unearthed distant relatives of the road alligator. Some science-mongers are mystified that they have not been able to trace its ancestry. They are also upset that the discovery of such a ubiquitous animal was by a virtual neophyte in the field of science-mongering.

The discovery of the road alligator is attributed to a little-known naturalist named Halfa Buck. She had a less-than auspicious reputation in the field of purist naturalism because she hadn't been educated in the structure of naturalism as were so many of her contemporaries. She was a natural at naturalism by her very nature. This was upsetting to those naturalists who had spent so many years learning to be naturalists. While the other naturalists were being schooled in the structure of naturalism, Halfa gained knowledge of the subject through personal experience. She did not have the luxury of the funding it took to go to school to get a certificate in naturalism. Although renowned as the foremost authority on road alligators, her beginnings were humble.

Like many misguided youths, she had no plans for her future and didn't know what career she would enjoy. Twelve grueling years of school did not leave her with enough skills to strike out, or, it could be said, left her with few enough skills to strike out in any field. She needed more education. When she applied at the local community college, the guidance counselor told her that she would need at least four years of remedial classes before being able to take courses toward a four-year degree. She realized that must mean, um, six more years of school just to get a four-year degree. In calculating this, what with a remedial Masters program, then the regular Masters program, then the remedial Doctorate, and the regular Doctoral work, she might never finish school. The situation seemed impossible. She calculated that the alternatives were equally as bad. Why, working forty hours per week at a wage of $5.00 per hour would get her, uh, only $180.00.

In need of income, she embarked on a life of selling her favors.

THE BIG BOOK OF DAN

This was the only viable means of support an insufficient education left her.

Not knowing the business, she started at the bottom. She became an alley walker. Her keen natural ability and talent soon resulted in a promotion to streetwalker. Her drive and ambition propelled her past avenue walker all the way to highway walker in only four short years.

Halfa's career as a highway walker resulted in her being placed in some precarious positions. On several occasions, she was accosted, cajoled, waylaid, abused, and generally mistreated by monopeds, bipeds, tripeds, and quadrupeds of various species, from human to animal. When she finally decided on naturalism as her chosen field, certain prejudices swayed her decision as to what specific area of this expansive field she would labor in. The one creature she encountered regularly that had never bothered her was the road alligator. On occasion, the road alligator actually befriended her and helped her out of some tight spots.

One occasion that Halfa appreciatively and repeatedly recounted was the unfortunate incident that ended up with her being chased down the berm late one Thursday night. Her pursuers were a one-legged female companion of a truck driver and a rather ferocious three-legged Shit Zoo (pronounced Shih Tzu). It all began with an innocent comment by Halfa about her favorite song, "At the Hop."

With all of the excitement, Halfa had a hard time getting a firm grasp on the sequence of events. But she was positive that while running for her life from this crazy woman with that yapping dog, a large bull road alligator sprang from nowhere, felling the crazy woman. Whatever the circumstances, Halfa was grateful. She made a secret pact with herself to learn more about these unassuming creatures and to help them.

After her success in the field of highway walking had lost its magic, she knew the time had come to move on. Craving to make a name for herself, she chose the field that interested her most: naturalism. It seemed logical to do something related to the state in which she spent most of her time.

Ms. Buck began her career as a naturalist based on the shaky credentials of being the daughter of a once famous great white hunter, "bring 'em back alive Frank Buck," and an East Indian chamber girl, Changefora. This, she felt, would give her at least a bit of credence with those more schooled in the field. These credentials, never substantiated, are believed to be false.

The implied experience of being reared by people connected with the natural world seemed to add validity to her interest in the natural world, or at least Halfa thought so. Another fact stressed in her defense was the existence of a renowned organization known as the Autobahn Society, a recognized authority in the field of naturalism. If a bunch of German highway walkers were recognized, then certainly room existed for her, too. Convoluted as this reasoning may have been, it provided the foundation for her study of the natural world.

Without government grants or outside support from any organization, she decided to live among the animals that interested her so much. She wanted to learn their habits and someday publish a comprehensive book about them. If successful, she would give lectures and educate the peoples of the world about this little-known animal.

Unfortunately for Halfa, her work neared completion when a large, rogue male road alligator attacked her. Although wounded, she survived the incident. Sadly for the world, she lost her memory and, along with it, the manuscript she had begun.

In rehabilitation, Halfa never wholly regained her memory. Flashes of road life still lingered, and her therapists decided she should retrain as a truck driver. She felt most comfortable in that environment. After successful retraining, she went to live among the truckers. She took the name of Jane Goodhaul and finished out her life on the highway that she so dearly loved.

The manuscript was lost forever, and perhaps no one will ever be able to compile so extensive a document on road alligators again. Although some zoological studies have followed, the prevalent

THE BIG BOOK OF DAN

habits of the road alligator remain unrecorded. Amateur naturalists have gleaned some interesting facts from close observation in the wild; however, these observations exist only in undocumented form. Nevertheless, their consistency suggests authenticity. I present some of these observations here.

It is known that a road alligator is docile unless provoked. It usually remains in its home territory, resting comfortably during the daylight hours. The males, exclusively, nurture the young alligators. When observing this, you will usually notice a large adult male with young close by. The large male road alligator is known to lash out at invaders wandering into its territory. Should a passing car get too close to a road alligator, it will attack the undercarriage of the offending vehicle, causing extensive damage. The alligator defends its territory by wildly flailing its large tail in a whipping motion.

The migration of the road alligator is one of the most amazing feats of natural adaptation ever witnessed. If you ever have the privilege of viewing this phenomenon, you will begin to understand how marvelous this animal is. No one fully understands where the road alligator's winter habitat is located. Its range is yet to be determined, but it is believed to spread across the southern states during the cold months. The animal cleverly wraps itself around the tires of trucks and cars. Remarkably, it takes on the appearance of actual tire tread. As it approaches its birthing grounds, it readies itself by loosening its grip on the tire. At an appropriate moment, it springs from the tire to take up residence on the berm.

The feeding habits of the road alligator are still not understood as of this writing. The common supposition is that they are nocturnal feeders. It is unclear if they are omnivores, herbivores, carnivores, or just fussy eaters, but no sightings of food ingestion have ever been recorded.

(You may question the validity of the above information or the veracity of the witnesses to this phenomenal creature, but they are as

BERM BINGO

much a fact of nature as the merge (mer' gee). The merge was a native of France inadvertently imported into the States after the Second World War. The merge is a shovel-headed, two-tailed snake that lurks around the freeway cloverleaf. The warning signs are posted to motorists. Although unseen, the merge is a fact of nature. We have all witnessed the wild swerving of cars when approaching cloverleaf formations, all to avoid the dreaded merges. Seldom visible to the naked eye, all smart motorists know they are a danger.. And just as those in the know are fully aware of the merges, they also know of, and believe in, the road alligator.)

Be cautious in your identification while playing **Berm Bingo** because road alligators do look remarkably like tire treads. Should such a misidentification occur, points may be lost.

These two pictures will help you discern the differences between road alligators and the common tire tread. This, of course, is a truck tire tread.

◄ THE BIG BOOK OF DAN

This is a large bull road alligator. If you study the picture closely, you will see the subtle differences between the two very similar photos.

The Highway
(As It Has Replaced the River in the Human Psyche)

> I was born upon thy bank, river,
> My blood flows in thy stream,
> And thou meanderest forever
> At the bottom of my dream.
>
> Henry David Thoreau (1817-62)

> They're busy making bigger roads,
> and better roads and more,
> so that people can discover
> even faster than before
> that everything is everywhere alike.
>
> Piet Hein (b. 1905)

MEANDERING IN THE Atlantic Ocean brought the Europeans to the New World. Once they discovered this bountiful land, the new colonists established major settlements close to suitable harbors. This allowed delivery of life-sustaining goods, from the Old World to the New, by ocean-going vessels. Colonists were not successful at surviving on the foods indigenous to this new land. Many of the early settlements did not survive the winters. Shipments of goods were sporadic at best, and many settlers died between the first snow and the next spring. This took the excitement out of moving to a new land. Because of this connection between waterways and survival, all of the major cities that sprang up during subsequent periods were established and prospered on seaports, large navigable lakes, or rivers that could bear boat traffic. This was the only viable way to carry large cargoes and would remain so for many years to come. Looked upon as secondary to the distribution of supplies, roads were nothing more than paths worn in the compacted dirt made barren from frequent travel by wagons and horses. The hinterlands, far from the cities of commerce, remained attractive only to the economically disadvantaged, religious fanatics, hermits, and outlaws. This scenario persisted until the invention of the internal combustion engine and its adaptation to the automobile.

The automobile had its beginnings as a toy for the wealthy, a luxury too expensive for the masses. The masses were relegated to traveling by foot power or horse drawn vehicles. Henry Ford harnessed the assembly line to produce an inexpensive automobile for the public, employing those very people to whom he intended to sell vehicles. The inception of the mass- produced vehicle made it possible to carry goods further from the cities. The waterways, once so important to commerce, now took on a lesser role. The common perception of the waterway as the sustaining medium of transport waned.

Reared in a city connected to Lake Erie and aware of the Great Lakes as a means of transporting cargo to the industrialized North, I understood the traditions of this type of life. I did not realized the unimportance of water travel to people not connected with it until I moved away from Cleveland.

The usual route from Fort Wayne, Indiana to Cleveland, Ohio is the Indiana Toll Road to the Ohio Turnpike, which leads directly to Interstate 480. Although not the shortest route, it is certainly the fastest. I mention this particular route because I often traveled it. I had many hours to study it and watch its development.

Sometime in the mid-eighties a development of yuppie castles rose up just outside of Toledo, next to a golf course, bordering the easement along the Turnpike. As I watched it grow, I marveled at the grand style of those houses. Why so near the dust, fumes, and the whining sound of rubber on asphalt? Why would anyone want to

THE HIGHWAY (AS IT HAS REPLACED THE RIVER IN THE HUMAN PSYCHE)

live on property backed up to the despised four-lane? This anomaly led me to question my perceptions, which no longer seemed valid. Something had changed so subtly that I had missed it. For some reason not yet revealed to me, the four-lane mysteriously enhanced future homeowning. It had become desirous not to behold the pristine snow falling on the wide expanse of one's lawn. The new view, a procession of travelers mucking through dingy slush, was in vogue. Forced to evaluate my perception of the 'wonderful life,' I questioned the logic at work here.

On one particular trip, squirming in my seat, fidgeting with the radio trying to find a station and again noticing the pretentious mansions, the rationale crystallized. On the bridge over the Maumee River between Exits 4 and 5 of the Ohio Turnpike, Eureka! I realized the answer.

Although the waterway had lost its place as the wellspring of existence, in subsequent generations the road had taken its place. The Interstate had become the artery of sustenance in the psyche of man, who now sought to be close to this valuable resource. Accomplished subtly over the years, it was unnoticeable to me until I viewed the river from the highway bridging it. This view coupled the two images into one single thought, clarifying the connection between our society and the ever-increasing subordination to ground transportation as a vital link to survival. It is a done deal, not to be changed, until we run out of the power to propel us down those concrete and asphalt byways. The system is attributed to President Eisenhower.

The Eisenhower/Interstate connection was first revealed to me on a stretch of Interstate 70 outside Indianapolis. Historic roadway markers spelled out the story for those interested enough to stop and read them. Compulsive readers know of these aluminum markers found along the highway, painted dark blue with raised silver lettering. They give the impression that our forefathers were thoughtful enough to have every historic event happen at the site of a rest area. Perhaps the pioneers of highway design routed us to meander through the countryside following the historic happenings outlined on the markers.

However it happened, it is a convenient history lesson provided for the hungry, bleary-eyed traveler.

Remembering the information on the marker, President Eisenhower (then Lieutenant Eisenhower) graduated from West Point in 1915. Second Lieutenant Eisenhower was assigned the command of a convoy traveling from the east to the west coast. Using the inadequate roads of the time, the journey took three months to complete. As his ass bumped along on the seat, with miles of two-lane cow paths ahead, he realized how important a good highway system could be to our national defense. The Federal-Aid Highway Act of 1944 created the National System of Interstate and Defense Highways. It was not until "Ike" obtained passage of the massive public works project that the work on our highway system began in earnest.

It seems clear that all government decisions arise in similar fashion. A prodding of the posterior is the only motivation to which our elected officials seem to respond. Lieutenant Eisenhower's trip from coast to coast took three months, in which time his firm resolution to improve our highway system was prodded from posterior to posterity.

Our Interstate Highway System, officially named the National Systems of Interstate and Defense Highways, is a network of multiple-lane, limited-access expressways authorized by the Federal Government. In 1990, the system was reported 99.2% complete. It consisted of 42,400 miles of highway. That it is part of our National Defense Strategy is important when considering the following information.

Approximately five years after the beginning of the Interstate Highway system (no one knows for sure) an organization, or gang, was formed to carry out destructive activities against the road-building project in an effort to disrupt or even discontinue the progress. They consistently took terrorist actions against the highway system. The public is unaware of these covert actions. Because the highway system is part of the National Defense Strategy, the existence of this organization has been kept a closely guarded secret by all government agencies from federal down to local levels. The insidious nature

THE HIGHWAY (AS IT HAS REPLACED THE RIVER IN THE HUMAN PSYCHE)

of the organization and its ability to strike undetected has left the Federal Government agencies (FBI and CIA) in total disarray in attempts to combat their actions.

The organization has chosen over these many years not to reveal itself or lay claim to many destructive activities. Its purpose is obscure. It was felt at one time that the organization was part of a Communist plot. With the RED MENACE begging for capitalism, it is now believed it may be an environmental group. Another emerging view is that it started out as communist but, with the fall of the ideology, switched to environmentalism. Whatever the case, we may never know the true meaning or purpose of its random acts of destruction. However, the evidence of its existence is overwhelming, and it should not be ignored.

The average motorist traveling on America's highways will see evidence of the organization's existence. The typical tactic is to wait until heavy traffic periods such as summer tourist season or holidays and then to strike without warning. Seemingly overnight, it will destroy large sections of highway or bridges to disrupt travel. The government, in order to maintain secrecy, will claim these incidents to be road improvement projects. When interviewing frequent travelers about the "improvements," they reveal that two days previous, the stretch of highway in question was in good condition. In urban areas, traffic is always heavy and the terrorist activity is daily. When traveling in places such as Chicago or LA, you can personally attest to this. How many times have you traveled a highway daily only to one day suddenly find a series of roadblocks and barricades accompanied by flashing warnings.

Its use of protest signs supports the hypothesis that in recent years this group is connected to environmentalist activities. The organization chooses to place these signs down the road from the destruction, allowing motorists to witness the full impact of the devastation. In the simplest of messages, they make their demands known. Large black letters against an iridescent orange background demand, "END CONSTRUCTION." Because this is an issue of national defense the demand goes unheeded, and building goes on.

If we appreciate "America the Beautiful" as it is today, threaded with 42,400 miles of Interstate, we owe homage to President Eisenhower. His thoughtful effort allowed the auto industry to accelerate to its position of dominance and a way of life for America and the world.

The highway is definitely the new river of commerce, the arterial network connecting one industrial heart to another. It has definitely and permanently replaced the waterway as the conveyor of necessities and made possible the expansion to previously inaccessible areas reserved for hermits and outcasts. No longer restricted by the earth's natural formations, we the children of Mother Earth are free to wander from the womb, umbilical cord snipped, in our gas-powered perambulators, suckled on the multi-colored teat of the gas pump.

Long ago, the highway was considered a strip on which to drive your (pleasure-craft) automobile. With the birth of each new generation, the idea of highway and automobile as a necessity became more deeply ingrained in our collective subconscious. This phenomenon has created more than one new industry and has allowed this seed of invention to blossom far beyond any expectations of its early pioneers.

Automobile manufacturing has developed into a super-sophisticated industry as witnessed by attending an auto show in Detroit recently. The car is marketed as an important component in every phase of our existence from birth to death. As it will carry you home from the hospital after transporting your pregnant mother there, it will also carry your decrepit carcass to the grave after a life spent as a devoted consumer and user.

This is how it all begins:

Upon discharge from the hospital, you are swaddled in an ultra-modern, extremely safe, car seat. You are then transported to the garage (a protective shelter for the car) by the current operator of the vehicle. To the amazement of your squinty little eyes, they had

THE HIGHWAY (AS IT HAS REPLACED THE RIVER IN THE HUMAN PSYCHE)

the foresight to attach a building, called a house, to the garage. This house is designed to be a waiting area so you have a comfortable place to stay until your next excursion in the car.

As you grow, your feet get closer to the pedals. You are waiting anxiously to press them. You spent years watching all of those exciting commercials. Cars crashing, swerving, climbing mountains, cars as scenes of sexual encounters, vacation freedoms, and all of the pleasures of being able to drive. In the interim, the car operators who stay in the house with you, known as your Partially Aware Resource for Entertainment, Nutrition, and Transportation, or PARENTs for short, have provided you with pseudo-cars with which to practice. They have also provided, through action and example, the firm conviction that without one you would be doomed to a mundane existence, and the joyous benefits associated with ownership would not be yours.

Finally the day comes. It is your turn to own and operate the coveted vehicle known as "my car" and to embark upon the many miles of Ike's dream.

Up to this time in your life, others had always chosen the car. If you could use a car at all, it was Mom's old minivan or Dad's four-door rust-bucket, but now the choice is finally yours.

The Marketing Department at the "Big Three" has also been planning for this glorious day. All those years of glitzy commercials and magazine adds, the little messages sent out about the rapture you are going to experience, are about to pay off. The "Big Three" stand ready to deliver your super-charged, brightly colored, sports model with the tiny back seats that those ignorant, old bastards who live with you cannot crawl into or out of.

That's okay because Dad will be busy adding on to the garage for the new vehicle and Mom will be busy keeping fresh clothes ready for your next return home. After all, you can't afford to move into a place of your own for at least the next five years because of the car insurance payments.

You now have that feeling of freedom guaranteed to you by all of those years of advertisements, a feeling that you will treasure all of

◄ **THE BIG BOOK OF DAN**

your life, until at age 83 you are no longer able to read road signs or navigate safely. At that time, the State Department of Motor Vehicles will strip you of your driver's license and along with it the freedom associated with driving, all this leaving you with a cold, bitter feeling. Until then, you are a lifelong target for the marketing wizardry of the auto manufacturers. They are continually busy planning your next move.

The female child will allow Dad to pick out her car; after all, he knows about such things and has spent many hours convincing her of his natural male mechanical talents. She will have the nice mid-size, mid-priced convertible in an ambrosial pastel blue with a white interior.

Of course, Sonny ain't buying that crap. After all, engine size is directly related to organ size, a fantasy all males cling to and one that is well advertised. Color is also important. None of those sissy colors for him; he needs a color that makes a statement, such as blood red or jet black. Only two doors are needed, and a back seat just big enough to two torsos with intertwined legs, would be a plus. As long as speed and looks are right, why should price matter? The right image helps catch women. Paradoxically, as the male is busy trying to catch women, he ends up being caught.

At this stage, those marketing wizards are ready again to take on the challenge of supplying your next vehicle, the Family Car.

Please keep in mind that you are part of a well-defined, well-developed system. Although you may say that this is not true, and for some at certain stages it may not be true, eventually you will be plugged into the system. If you are having trouble swallowing this fact, ask yourself, where are the hippies of the Sixties, the idealists who were going to change the world? They may have skipped the first stage of car consumerism, but eventually they arrived at the next stage, the Family Car, and continued down the path to the final stages.

The Family Car is a device to carry you and the products of your unplanned, errant sexual passions of the Hot Rod phase further down the road of life. The Family Car is the shiny new vehicle parked in

THE HIGHWAY (AS IT HAS REPLACED THE RIVER IN THE HUMAN PSYCHE)

front of the shiny new house in which live those shiny newlyweds and those shiny-faced kids. Family Car purchasing may go through various stages, but each stage is similar. Although size changes may be required, it is usually a vehicle of substantial utility and practicality, as well as moderate cost. (There are certainly the aberrations of the neurotic, clinging to past glory that forces the family of six to pack into the sports car, but that is well outside the norm).

The pleasure of purchase is always keen, and pride of ownership is high. However, because of the high usage rate, it soon becomes the Rust Bucket, a monument to your frustration, strewn with candy wrappers, carpeted in chewing gum, upholstered in cigarette burns, and defaced with dents, dings, and scratches.

Now those future drivers, who sprang from your long since dormant passions, come of age. Memories of speed, sex, pleasure, and freedom creep back to beguile your aging mind. Across the room from you, your wife dreams of something she can call her own. She is dreaming of a car minus the smell of ammoniated diapers, popcorn, dogs, or kids.

This stage of vehicularism presents a dilemma for the sales forecaster. At this point, the divergent tastes of the consumer are based on want, rather than need. What...the hell...do they want, anyway? Some want speed, some want peace of mind, some have price in mind, others comfort. But for certain consumers, rugged "outdoorsy" is most appealing. The balding, pony-tailed tycoon in his second childhood may choose a sports car with a price tag that screams success. He desires the perfect vehicle to go strumpet hunting in. He craves a vehicle that shows all those young women just what kind of equipment he has. If he is still attached to a mate, he may even buy a matching one for her. Usually, however, the house-weary mother of his children is relegated to driving the last vestige of the 'Family Car' as part of the divorce settlement, should the sports car lead to successful strumpet hunting.

The middle-aged woman who has survived the temporary insanity of her husband's dalliances may choose, as part of her reward, a luxury model or a foreign sports model. The choice of a minivan or station wagon will be far from her mind. This is a knee jerk reaction and a survival instinct, factoring in future grandchildren.

The person caught in the rugged individualist drama may picture himself in a 4 X 4 sports model, speeding down the highway toward the mountains with the city skyline visible through oversized side mirrors. The individualist's dream-come-true is a freshly killed deer strapped to the front fender and a boat in tow, visible through the gun rack in the rear window. This knobby-tired, jacked-up model is a tribute to the expertise of those advertising geniuses who have convinced the driver that, although his entire life is spent watching TV and participating in life only vicariously through the TUBE, by driving this vehicle to the grocery to get his Doritos everyone will think he is Tarzan reincarnated. The only activity these drivers usually experience is the exertion of climbing into the driver's seat located four feet off the ground. I believe this to be a popular image for many. Every time I come out of the grocery there is one parked next to me. Backing out of my space becomes a bit of a wilderness adventure in itself. The manufacturers should supply these vehicles with a porthole at normal level so poor guys like me can look through to see if anything is going to hit them as they pull out.

For those who can't make a decision, there are the four-car garages built with appropriately-sized, attached houses. These structures are grouped in subdivisions so that one can live next to other vehicle owners of the same magnitude. These subdivisions usually back up to the four-lane, close to the sights, sounds, and smells that reinforce the idea that ownership of multiple vehicles is the most necessary aspect of life. Owning only one vehicle would be inexcusable. It leaves you open to problems of mechanical failure, a vehicle unsuitable for current weather condition, or showing up for an event in an inappropriate vehicle. All or any of these might lead to disenfranchisement from your four-car community.

Don't worry though, the manufacturers and their representatives have all of the possibilities covered for you. The types and sizes of

THE HIGHWAY (AS IT HAS REPLACED THE RIVER IN THE HUMAN PSYCHE)

cars and the options available will satisfy your every desire. The days of one type, one size, and one color are long gone. The choices available today would have petrified the buyer of only a few years ago, but with everything riding on your decision, you must find ample time to research the options.

When this characteristic middle-age stage of indecision has passed, car ownership once again becomes a cut-and-dried situation. Your tired old body cries out for comfort. It needs to be cradled in a seat that doesn't jostle you up and down or toss you from door to console at every turn. It is now time for the ultimate in belligerence and showmanship. One day you wake up, put your teeth in, toupee on, and head to the Cadillac dealer. If you are at a stage prior to this, you may laugh and scoff at the idea. You may believe that at thirty you have already reached the ultimate Volvo Experience. You may proclaim that Cadillac is not the ultimate in automobile one-upmanship. This will pass. When you reach pre-senility, you will realize Cadillac is not a car; it is a state of mind.

The Cadillac idea has already been planted in your subconscious. Through years of subliminal messages beamed at you from the bowels of the marketing department of General Motors, it is in some dark, yet undiscovered, corner of your mind. One morning you will wake with only one thought: I need a Cadillac.

Cadillac is the vehicle that propels you down the four-lane at 35 mph. As people pass you with middle fingers waving furiously, you will know with complete confidence that you have led your life properly. This model allows you to attain the highest pinnacle of car ownership.

Cadillac is the statement of status that permits you to pass at 50 mph in school zones and that gives you the right to take up two lanes of the road and three parking spaces at the grocery store.

Cadillac is symbolic of the time between old age and death when you deserve the rewards for all the previous make-due vehicles that weren't quite Cadillacs.

At this time, you deserve the ultimate in comfort and posh surroundings while you are being a pain in the ass to pedestrians and the rest of the driving public. With the luxurious rolled and pleated interior and rich appointments, it is like a pre-coffin, a staging area for your next long, quiet, eternal ride. Cadillac is what carries you finally in a cold, prone position to your resting place, just off the four-lane. Cadillac transports your grieving family behind you, engrossed in the tactical discussion about who is going to get the new Cadillac you ordered the week before your demise.

Yes, the marketing departments of those automobile manufacturers have been busy planning car purchasing for your entire life. They have an unspoken duty to keep you on those highways.

The automotive industry is the single largest influence on the world economy, and without it, the entire world economy would be in shambles. Mobility is the single most important condition to survival, and it all depends on miniscule sea creatures that became extinct millions of years ago. When we have finished sucking the last bit of oil out of the ground, we may end up as the next oil deposit, but until then, the burgeoning industries continue to grow out of our mobility.

At the Off Ramp (Or the Homogenization of Our Society)

"You got to be careful if you don't know where you're going, because you might not get there."

- Yogi Berra

THE MOTEL IS an example of a business directly related to the car and its occupants. People have long bragged about how many consecutive hours they drove to reach their destination. There are those unfortunate times when the destination is too far to travel in one sitting, and passenger mutiny is at hand. To accommodate travelers, the motor hotel, later shortened to the motel, was invented.

In the early years following their inception, motels were small, unsophisticated, homey enterprises. They often consisted of just a few bungalows or a row of partitioned-off rooms in a common building. The rooms were only a little larger than the car you rode in all day. As the car became more sophisticated and dependable, long distance travel became more popular. The motel of the era soon became too small to accommodate all the travelers. With the advent of the four-lane, these motels were now far off the most popular routes. Motels, to fill the needs of this new generation of travelers, needed to be more sophisticated, more accessible, and comprehensive enough to provide all necessary services in one location.

An entrepreneur with as much vision as Henry Ford created the Holiday Inn to fulfill this need. The word "standardization" became all-important. No matter where you traveled, the Holiday Inn would have ready for you the same room you left the day before. It was great; you could leave Wichita in the morning, travel all day, and check into a room that looked exactly like the one you left that morning. Recently, standardization is not as desirable. The swing is back to individualism, but with a high level of sophistication. Motels now offer as many levels of sophistication as the car companies, everything from the small economy room to the "Cadillac room" with all of the accessories you had to leave out in the parking lot in your real Cadillac.

Another marvelous contraption of our mobile society evolved into what is known today as the recreational vehicle. Called a travel trailer when I was young, I don't remember ever seeing one in our neighborhood. They were certainly in existence; I do remember seeing one in a Laurel and Hardy movie. Although available, travel trailers were far too impractical for families owning one used car that had enough trouble propelling itself down the road, without the added burden of dragging a household behind.

The explosion of the Recreational Vehicle industry must have taken place in the Sixties when liquid cash for families also exploded. Whatever the chronological evolution of the recreational vehicle, it has enhanced the ability to travel down those four-lanes. Certainly putting your whole house on wheels, pumping it full of gas and meandering from RV park to RV park has to be living life to its fullest. And it sure takes care of not liking your neighborhood. If you can't stand your neighbor, you just turn the key and press down on the accelerator.

About five years ago on a trip to Florida, while searching for the wintering grounds of the Road Alligator, the number of recreational vehicles on the highway astounded me, and even more so, the combinations of the things they had in tow. They were reminiscent of wagon trains of the 1800's. Of course, there were cars towing trailers, trucks towing trailers and motor homes towing cars, but these were the simple combinations. The addition of boats, motorcycles, utility trailers, and miscellaneous items made the combinations endless. The winner had to be the guy driving a Winnebago with a motorcycle strapped to the back, towing a car with two bicycles in a rack on the roof, with a motor boat attached to the back bumper of the car, and a rowboat strapped to the top of the motor boat.

AT THE OFF RAMP (OR THE HOMOGENIZATION OF OUR SOCIETY)

For those pioneer spirits who have chosen this way of life, the four-lane is certainly a necessity. For people who travel by RV, another necessity is the RV park. It is never more than a culvert away from the roadside. The brightly colored outhouses, pumping stations, and souvenir stores all cluster around a small lake. Each available vehicle space fills with a shiny trailer full of happy campers, communing with nature, all within 100 yards of the beloved four-lane.

The RV industry has grown over the years, and during this growth, it has had to appeal to many varied tastes, just as the automobile industry has done. There are many grades of recreational vehicles. The pop-up tent style is on the low end, designed for the young family just starting out; next is the model that mounts on the bed of your pickup truck, and so on up the line until you reach the tow-behind. The ultimate in recreational vehicles is the self-contained unit that looks remarkably like a bus for two. This is the Cadillac of motor homes. I would be wary of passing the person driving to Florida in one of these monstrous vehicles and towing a real Cadillac. The mentality particular to this combination has to be double thick. This driver would probably be so steeped in "Cadillacism" that he wouldn't let you pass anyway.

The RV practitioners do draw some parallels to the pioneers of old with their modern versions of the prairie schooner, be they ever so faint. Perhaps the more fitting parallel to the pioneers is the motorcyclist. The top of the heap in motor cycle riding, if not in fact, then at least in perception, is the Harley rider. The Harley Davidson motor cycle company has taken an organization on the verge of failure, and through product improvement and a tremendous marketing plan, elevated it to a status symbol. This in itself is amazing, but credit should go to a less likely group than the marketing executives at Harley Davidson. The dreaded Hell's Angels, who rose to prominence in the 60's, created the look, mystique, and desire for the Harley. The Harley riders of today are the modern version of the pioneer, cowboy, and outlaw all rolled into one, or at least they try to look the part.

THE BIG BOOK OF DAN

You cannot just ride a Harley to be a Harley rider; you have to dress the part. If you don't properly accessorize, it doesn't count. Basic black is a must. The fashion is jeans with black chaps, black boots with the mid-height heels, black leather jacket (or for the more casual occasion, the denim shirt with black leather vest) and a red kerchief worn either on the head or around the neck. As always, the jewelry should be simple silver with turquoise stones. Facial hair and ponytails are not a must but a plus to the overall look. Please do not ride a Harley dressed in a suit or even your casual wear; this is not only offensive, but you may be viewed as some sort of pervert, or worse yet, a thief. Should you be mistaken for a thief, the consequences could be fatal. These modern cowboys view the Harley as a steed. You might suffer similar punishment to the horse thief of cowboy lore, and you might even be hanged for the offense. (Does it sometimes seem to you that life has turned into a costume party? And you never have the right costume!)

By far the most amazing outgrowth of our highway society is the ever-expanding, one-stop-wonder, the truck stop. The diversity of services these stops offer has steadily increased over time. When first begun, the main features were gas, water, and service for your vehicle, with the convenience of food while you waited. From these humble beginnings, a shopping mall and service center for the traveler's personal needs have arisen, along with the convenience of vehicle service. There seems to be an undeclared war among gas companies vying to develop the ultimate truck stop. I believe the current leader is in Iowa. This particular location is billed as the largest truck stop in the country. Wow! Wouldn't that be the ultimate destination for your next vacation?

Truck stop is a misnomer. It has far outgrown the original meaning. A new term needs to be coined to catch the full flavor of the modern Truck Stop. The modern Truck Stop offers the following: a restaurant, barber shop, bank, clothing store, grocery store, bathing facilities, jewelry, games, books, greeting cards, hair dressers, massage (therapeutic only), podiatry, dentistry, pharmaceuticals, marriage

AT THE OFF RAMP (OR THE HOMOGENIZATION OF OUR SOCIETY)

counseling, and, in isolated instances, psychiatric services. Of course, a motel goes without saying, and rows and rows of fuel pumps provide that required essence of motor travel. Yes sir, the Truck Stop has grown into the handiest dandiest place on earth. The corporate giants of fuel have made the oasis so inviting, running low on gas is now a good thing.

Although the Truck Stop image has undoubtedly improved, I have noticed some yet to be explained oddities. I can only suspect that a secret, unspoken-of service lurks in this haven for tired travelers. In the men's restroom, you will find a curious little machine. This machine dispenses cologne for a quarter. Yes! You may purchase, for the price of two bits, such scents as Polo or Dakar to splash on liberally. From another dispenser on the same wall, for thrice the price, you may purchase protection from the little bugs that can kill you. Once used to prevent life, now billed as a device to save lives, the mighty condom is available.

The condom machine has been sterilized to portray the new Fortune 500 image of the modern mobile world. The big names in fuel and lubrication can feel comfortable about having them affixed to the walls of their new-image establishments. The machine of old had three compartments, each filled with some style or shape of thrill as depicted in a bawdy picture along with a clever caption on the front of the machine. A sterilized version has replaced these machines, a mechanical drug store often including slots for stomach medicine, headache medicine, and a very basic condom without ribs, bumps, flashing lights, flavors, or exotic colors. The choices are curious. If she turns your stomach or has a headache, you can combat these maladies and still have safe sex for only three times the total of three quarters.

Standing at the urinal with these machines in front of me, I wonder if a woman is offered the same choices. Is there a perfume dispenser spritzing out Jungle Passion for only three quarters? Does she view a lubrication station oozing out metered quantities of KY jelly or spermicidal cream? Does a similar machine offer her stomach medicine, headache medicine, and perhaps crotchless panties attractively embroidered with the truck stop's logo or the state emblem across the seat to help recall fond memories?

This all enhances the theory that your home on the road is looking after your every driving need. The servicing of those physical desires, as once portrayed in fables of bawdy seaport and river town houses, is now available right out there on the highway. If you are lucky enough to find a welcoming port, the harbormaster is concerned that you might get barnacles on your dinghy. He has provided the proper protective coating for you to prevent this.

Well, certainly you can see that all possible comforts are provided along your highway route, although I must admit that the statement that psychiatric services exist in some truck stops is not entirely true yet. But as you drive down these paths of progress, you will be convinced that there is a need for such services. For the modern dysfunctional family who cannot get along in a 4,000 square foot house, traveling from New York to California may require a smattering of counseling, say in Kansas or so. The modern mobile serial killer would not have gone so wrong if a bit of advice had been given in Oklahoma as he was gassing up to meet his next victim. These may be extreme cases, but who knows!

People traveling down highways give the impression of being little portable countries. So great is the feeling of independence, they become anarchists, self-rulers of their little tin islands, aggressors gobbling up land as if it were a permanent conquest, acting as though it will all be theirs, rather than acting as mere drivers trying to reach a destination. If you keenly observe people as they travel, you will note some interesting behavior, behavior that seems very competitive in a non-competitive situation. Behavior that doesn't appear to be called for. No matter what speed you travel, there are always drivers willing to speed past you as if there is an undeclared race. You have been designated a competitor without being notified.

Why do people pass you even if you are going faster than the speed limit? Why do people pass you just to travel at the same speed you are going, or, worse yet, pass you and then slow down? I developed a theory for this behavior called The Four-Lane Theory of Superiority.

If you would like to get a pulse on who feels superior, travel down the four-lane at 5 mph over the speed limit and take note of who passes you. I say 5 mph over the speed limit for a reason: this is the speed usually traveled. Over the years, the knowledge that five over is the customary limit (a "given" by the highway patrol) has reinforced that as the unofficial speed limit. Going over this limit is considered speeding, and those who do so are taking a risk. Passing you gives them a feeling of superiority, even if it is fleeting and hinges on your willingness not to, in turn, pass them.

As these competitive motorists whiz by, they will take a brief instant to peer into your window to see whom they are getting ahead of and to allow you the opportunity to issue a challenge or cower under their might. Mechanical failure or the radar gun of local law enforcement reverses their superiority. Forced to sink into defeat, they again strike out even faster to rebel against the oppression. If only they had been given proper counseling at the truck stop, they may have been able to conquer the need to engage in this activity.

Enough of The Four-Lane Theory; you get the picture. On any road trip, you will see The Four-Lane Theory in action. All you need to gain superiority is a key and some gas, at least until lights flash and the czar of the highways, keeping the proletariat under control, pulls you over.

Many things have changed in the recent past concerning transportation. All of these changes have evolved from idea to invention to luxury to necessity, and they have served to alter the standard of living in the U.S. We base our prosperity on the supply of long-extinct animal life, which over thousands of years turned into oil. What happens when we run out? We are going to be left with some really neat jogging tracks!

◄ THE BIG BOOK OF DAN

This is an interesting billboard on the way to Oak Ridge Tennessee. It advertizes exotic dancers. This one apparently has three arms, which is quite exotic. Oak Ridge, Tennessee is the place the U.S. Government opened during World War II to develop nuclear weapons, and it has been a nuclear test facility ever since. The girl on the billboard is obviously a local girl from Oak Ridge.

Tennessee Driving Philosophies and Practices

An eerie sight, it could be from a Stephen King story. Four cars pulled up to a four-way stop, skeletons sitting behind the wheel, family Bible on the seat, key turned in the ignition, no gas in the tank, and dead batteries. Could this be an urban legend? Perhaps, but just maybe four Christians coming home from Wednesday night's prayer meeting trying to out-polite each other.

✦✦✦

SETTLING IN TENNESSEE as a Midwest transplant was not as big a shock as moving to Fort Wayne, Indiana, from Cleveland, Ohio. You might say that Fort Wayne provided a transitional move from big city to mid-sized city. Fort Wayne is similar in many respects to Knoxville. The demographics are alike, the city amenities are certainly equivalent, and the homogenization of customs and culture has certainly taken place, at least as much as possible. I enjoy living here and, although given the opportunity to relocate, I chose to stay in this amazing place.

My perception of the world is more impressionistic than factual. I prefer to make up my mind by observing rather than reading. I have arrived at conclusions about my Tennessee surroundings through experiencing and feeling my way. When I moved here, I was very much the tourist. I anticipated traveling to surrounding small towns and day-tripping to scenic destinations each weekend. Each trip yielded a sight or two not experienced in all my previous travels. For instance, sights like the majestic, old-growth tulip poplars on the trail to Ramsey's Cascade were unforgettable.

Along with the natural beauty of the Smokey Mountains, there is an abundance of small town charm and elegantly simple people brimming with tales of family and friends, willing to share of themselves with inquisitive strangers. Being from the land above the Mason Dixon, and caught off guard by the dialect to the point of embarrassment, I asked frequently for the repetition of words or phrases. To this end, I found stacks of books translating country speak into a less contracted structure understood by my Northern brain. There is, however, something I have never seen that would be more valuable to a tourist motoring through Tennessee than a quaint book on how to speak hillbilly. A book or pamphlet titled *The Philosophy of Driving in Tennessee* could effectively explain the nuances of motoring, as developed over years of going to Bible classes three days a week and attending a religious service on Sunday afternoon called NASCAR.

When I moved here, I noticed anomalies in the rules of the road. Because of the dichotomy of local folk and the Oak Ridge eggheads, I suspected the incongruity could be Newtonian. Newton postulated, "A body at rest tends to stay at rest, a body in motion tends to stay in motion." After considering that an automobile at 0 MPH is not actually at rest but waiting to transfer rotary motion into linear motion at the command of the operator, I gave up on this as a viable explanation. Upon further observation and weighty consideration of my experiences, I did reach conclusions concerning motor vehicle operation in Tennessee and the rules governing said operation:

1. The usual hard and fast rules of motor vehicle operation in other states are only for the uninformed tourists passing through Tennessee.
2. Vehicle operator decorum at 0 MPH is cancelled once forward motion is established.
3. There are actually no rules governing operation of moving vehicles. The signs and indicators are merely suggestions for operation of a motor vehicle and may be ignored as convenience dictates.

To clarify some finer points on motor vehicle operation, I offer the following information:

TENNESSEE DRIVING PHILOSOPHIES AND PRACTICES

The octagonal red sign with the large letters "STOP" is multifunctional. It usually indicates slowing to 15 MPH before executing your next maneuver, but in rare instances, it may be necessary to attain the 0 MPH condition, at which time the 0 MPH decorum must be practiced.

The 0 MPH decorum dictates that common belief in who has the right of way does not hold in instances of two-way or four-way pauses when cars are either facing each other or perpendicular, as well as in the most accursed situation when all four corners have cars in the 0 MPH condition. In this situation, all vehicles must wait an indeterminate period until someone flashes headlights to indicate that permission to go first has been given. In any situation where two vehicles or more are in the 0 MPH mode, it is necessary to practice restraint. Immediate flashing of lights after reaching the 0 MPH condition causes confusion as to your intent. This two-way or four-way stop decorum is the only at-rest suggestion in Tennessee motor vehicle operation.

In moving to a description of forward motion, suggestions of road signs are explained below.

The rectangular sign at the side of the road that states a limit, such as SPEED LIMIT 55, indicates the lower limit of speed allowed on that particular roadway. In many states, this is the upper limit, which explains the aggravating situation posed by the unknowing tourists or transplants from other states who clog our highways.

The inverted triangular sign, "YIELD," indicates increasing your speed to avoid the person heading toward you from another direction.

The diamond-shaped sign with two lines, one vertical and the other intersecting it perpendicularly, is an instruction to increase your speed in case someone is obeying the 15 MPH "STOP" suggestion from the perpendicular direction. A diamond-shaped sign with a vertical line intersected by a horizontal line indicates applying the brakes until you reach the 0 MPH condition and then following the 0 MPH decorum, unless it is clear that no other vehicles are close enough to collide with yours, in which case the 15 MPH "STOP" suggestion can be followed.

One road sign that is most helpful to the Tennessee motorist is similar to the board held up by the crew chief at NASCAR races. Their sign indicates various milestones of the race: when the driver should come in for tire changes, when it is time to refuel, and other necessities to assist in winning the race. The road sign on a four-lane highway stating the mileage to the next exit serves a similar purpose. A sign stating 1.0 miles to an exit allows the driver 0.975 miles to position himself in the far left lane and pass as many cars as possible before swerving through traffic to exit for fuel, potty breaks, food, or other services.

It can be surmised from its name alone that the traffic light should be given credence only if you are in a situation where there are sufficient vehicles to validate the term "traffic." Three important points to remember about these traffic lights are as follows: when red, the 15 MPH suggestion may be followed; when yellow, speed up sufficiently to avoid the red; when green, accelerate to a speed suitably over the minimum speed indicated on the "SPEED LIMIT" sign. Flashing yellow lights indicate a dangerous area. You need to *increase speed* when flashing yellow lights are seen and accelerate until well past the lights.

The development of our roadways occurred pre-NASCAR, so banked turns were unfortunately not incorporated into the highway system. To help Tennessee motorists navigate the highways, special additives have been added to the striping paint. Along with the suggested significance of the striping, special properties allow us to pilot twisty roads with relative ease as unwitting tourists swerve to miss us.

Let's review the suggested meaning of the striping and then the special paint properties. The striping paint used is either white or yellow. The colors are significant based on the degree of importance assigned to the suggestions. White lines are used when all the cars are going in the same direction. They have no special purpose and may be ignored at will. These lines are more useful than necessary. One use of the white dashed line is to better align your vehicle with

TENNESSEE DRIVING PHILOSOPHIES AND PRACTICES

the one in front of you so that you receive the full effect of drafting. *Drafting* is a maneuver used to cut wind resistance by getting within inches of the bumper of the car in front of yours. Drafting should not be confused with tailgating, a strictly Northern term. Tailgating is rude. Tailgating is following too close to the car in front of you for no apparent purpose. Drafting also affords you the ability to change lanes once a space of one car length opens next to you, one that is also demarcated by white dashed lines.

To the far right on some roads, you will notice a solid white line. This is the edge of the road. On certain roads, there is a full lane on the other side of that white line. This lane is the *emergency lane*, also known as the *special passing lane*. It is termed the emergency lane because it is suggested that you use it only when the other lanes are full of cars and you have important places to go.

Yellow lines are reserved for situations where caution needs to be exercised. Tourists and the uninformed are not familiar with the true meaning of these lines. Some vigilance is needed because these groups of people are a threat to the experienced Tennessee motorist. Long bursts of the horn are usually sufficient to get them out of your way. On rare occasions, you may need to slow slightly to allow them to witness your hand and finger gestures as you confront their ignorance.

The yellow lines on two-lane roads are easy to understand and important to follow. An oncoming vehicle, while you are traveling to the left side of the yellow line, may confront you. Many drivers fail to realize the importance of swerving out of your way, so it may be necessary to alter the direction of your trajectory. In these instances, it is completely acceptable to move abruptly to the right. Your vehicle may touch the vehicle to the right that you are displacing. This is completely acceptable. It is called *trading paint*, a well-respected tradition of driving in Tennessee.

The dashed yellow line is the simplest concept to grasp. It is similar to the dashed white line in as much as it demarcates two separate driving areas. The notable difference is that drivers approaching from the opposite direction will be using the same lanes, in the same manner.

◄ THE BIG BOOK OF DAN

The lane to the left of the line may be used to pass long lines of tourists traveling at the SPEED LIMIT and gawking as if they have never seen a tree before. This lane may also be used to drive in as long as you move to the right of the line within ten yards of cars traveling in the opposite direction.

A dashed line accompanied by a solid yellow line to the left of it denotes a section of road where you are allowed to use both lanes, but other drivers must use caution while you are left of the lines. This type of marking is more important to the people whom you are passing. This line serves as a warning that they must slow while you pass them if vehicles are coming from the other direction.

A solid line to the right of the dashed line offers a choice to the informed Tennessee motorist. You may pass cars that are going slower than you wish to travel, but you must do this at a high rate of speed. It is important to avoid motorists coming from the other direction who are following the suggestions stated in the above paragraph. Should this be inconvenient, you may have the availability of the emergency passing lane to the right, as explained above. Sounding your horn with one long burst should give the driver you are passing sufficient warning so he does not obstruct your passing.

The most challenging situation you will be confronted with will occur on stretches of road with solid, double yellow lines. These lines do not restrict your passing, but they challenge it. You will notice these lines appear on the twistiest, turniest parts of two-lane highways. The lines indicate to all drivers that they must be alert while you are passing them, and they must be willing to exert extreme pressure to the brake pedal should it become necessary. Experienced Tennessee motorists with equipment not up to the power of your machine are aware of this and are willing to exercise the necessary caution. Drivers less informed or jealous of your equipment may express resentment through vulgar hand gestures or obscene language. These people are showing their ignorance of traditional Tennessee motor vehicle practices.

As previously mentioned, the striping paint has special additives to help in negotiating Tennessee roads. Only the most perceptive

TENNESSEE DRIVING PHILOSOPHIES AND PRACTICES

Tennessee motorists are aware of the power of this paint, although more are becoming conscious of it as time passes. Still in the testing stages, the additive has only been used in yellow striping paint. It is applied exclusively to the centerlines and has a strong magnetic property. Motorists in the know will straddle the lines with the driver's side wheels until the ball joints are directly over the stripe. The magnetism of the stripes will effectively guide the car through turns and down straight stretches of road, allowing the driver time to text, dial cell phones, or put new discs in their CD player. Knowing motorists will allow for this, moving to the side of the road or into the special passing lane so as not to restrict such an accomplished motor vehicle operator's progress.

In closing, a new development in equipment has recently come to my attention. It is the introduction of special headlights. These lights have a repulsion beam feature not previously available to motorists. I have firsthand knowledge of the result of the beams, having experienced their effectiveness when used by a driver behind me. How the beam works is less mysterious to me than the operator possessing a vehicle with this feature. In theory, the beam works with your vehicle in the drafting position. Once in position, you turn on the bright lights. Leaving your bright lights on will mysteriously increase the speed of the car in front of you until it is traveling at a speed sufficient to satisfy your needs. The downside of this practice, if there is one, is that the lights illuminate the inside of their vehicle so that you must witness the resulting flailing of arms and facial contortions.

You will remember, as previously stated, that I have arrived at these conclusions through observation and deduction. All of the driving suggestions are apparently passed down through generations of driving tradition and are affected by changes in the NASCAR regulations developed over many years of trial and error. Because many people lose their lives to the Dale Earnhardt Syndrome, constant improvements are necessary to increase the awareness of those uninformed motorists traveling in Tennessee.

God bless your little heart, and happy motoring.

Rolling Down a Hill

cool pungent earth, tickle of grass
bright searing sun on my face
cool pungent earth, tickle of
bright searing sun on my
cool pungent earth, tickle
bright searing sun on
cool pungent earth
bright searing sun
cool pungent
bright searing
cool
bright
cool pungent
bright searing sun
cool pungent earth
bright searing sun on
cool pungent earth, tickle
bright searing sun on my
cool pungent earth, tickle of
bright searing sun on my face
lying in the meadow, stomach churning
when it stops I'll try again

More, More, More: People Need Less More and More Less

People need to be made more aware of the need to work at learning how to live because life is so quick and sometimes it goes away too quickly.

Andy Warhol (1928-87)

THIS ESSAY IS about observing and learning from people. Listening to and observing people provides and education unattainable elsewhere.

As the youngest child, I had two older brothers, Dave and Tom. Dave was firstborn and Tom two years older than I. While being raised, corporal punishment was still in effect. Dr. Spock did not receive the same credibility afforded to him years after our childhoods. I learned how to be an effective observer out of a need to survive the childhood experience without the welts and house arrests doled out to my brothers. They earned these for transgressions of the laws of our little social group. This was how I learned the importance of being a keen observer.

Being born third in the family is a greater advantage than any other position, as far as I can tell. The pecking order of a family runs from parents to first born and so on. For many of those early formative years, as Wonder Bread called them, I listened to and observed my brothers getting into trouble. Because they were older, their ability to find trouble outdistanced mine. I observed the punishments for the crimes, and when it was my turn, I knew what I could not afford to be caught at. I did everything they did; I just took the time to cover my tracks commensurate with the severity of the reprisal. Faced with the choice of pecking order, perhaps next time through, don't pick firstborn; it is a bad place to be. I found myself observing at an early age due to circumstance rather than wit. Observing has served me well. I am strongly in favor of listening and observing one's surroundings as a daily practice.

One of my first universal observations, outside of my family lessons, happened at the Sears and Roebuck store, when there still was a Roebuck. We lived on West 91 Street and Elmira Avenue in Cleveland. Sears was on West 110 Street and Lorain Avenue, well within walking distance from our neighborhood. It was not "The Mall" as is popular today, but it was a department store. It offered everything from clothes to tires, as they still do. The neighborhood gang made it a regular target because it was within walking distance and expansive enough to get away from the store detectives in crises. It was a marvelous place for an eight-year-old. It had a toy department! You could play for hours without being disturbed if you told the clerk your mom was dress shopping and had asked you to wait there for her. We seldom went there with our parents, and the dodge worked most of the time. Even if you were unfortunate enough to have to go with mom, she was never foolish enough to visit the toy department with you.

One area of the store was precious to us – the Arcade. The Arcade separated the automotive garage from the main store and acted as a barrier so that smells of grease, oil, and exhaust fumes did not enter the main part of the store. The Arcade housed The Pet Department, of little consequence to us. My father strictly forbad pets, and we had to share a neighborhood dog. The department next to the Pet Department we held in great awe and visited often: the Candy Department.

Dad did not subscribe to the concept of a weekly allowance, so the liquid cash available to us depended on grass growing or snow falling, both of which offered money-making opportunities. This unfortunate circumstance prevented us from being regular consumers, and we were relegated to window-shopping. However, they could not charge the smell of all of the chocolate, fresh roasted nuts, and popcorn. A regular visit just to take in those glorious aromas was well worth our time, and that is where I formulated a theory that still holds true today and is rapidly catching hold. I named it the POPCORN THEORY OF FAT.

MORE, MORE, MORE: PEOPLE NEED LESS MORE AND MORE LESS

The political correctness of calling someone fat was not considered when we were kids. Being overweight did not carry the stigma it carries today. We placed little concern on someone's size because there were very few fat people in our neighborhood. The range of sizes went from gaunt to slightly overweight. Obesity was an oddity treated with esteem, for some reason unknown to me at the time. In looking back at the reverence afforded corpulent people, it must have had something to do with affluence. Perhaps fat was an enviable condition denoting having enough money to get that way. When shopping day rolled around, the cupboards were bare at most houses in our neighborhood. Mom shopped for the essentials of existence, planning each meal with care. Although we had treats, they were sparse, and leftovers were seldom left over; they became part of tomorrow's meal.

One guy we always invited to play ball was Larry, the most overweight guy in the neighborhood. Larry had one advantage over everyone else. He always had a baseball or football we could use. He even had extra gloves and bats. Larry was affluent enough to have all that extra stuff. Larry was fat.

To get back to the Sears store and the Popcorn Theory of Fat, during the many visits to the Candy Department, I made a correlation between the size of the popcorn bag and the size of the purchaser, as well as his eating style.

The Candy Department had a machine to pop corn. The design of this machine not only popped the corn but also put irresistible smells into the air. The smells were so strong that they caused you to salivate as soon as they tickled your nose.

Life was different when I was a kid; you could smoke while doing your grocery shopping, and store policy permitted you to graze on popcorn while you perused the latest fashions. Many people made this their first stop on a trip through the store, a very busy place on a Saturday when the family car was available. Back then, most families only had one car.

Sears and Roebuck, in an effort to please every customer, offered

THE BIG BOOK OF DAN

a large selection of everything. This included popcorn containers. The sizes ranged from a small cylindrical-shaped bag you could barely get your hand into to a box about the size of a suitcase, complete with a set of carrying handles for the users' convenience. When we got up enough money to buy popcorn, we bought the small bag to conserve cash for other things. We envied anyone who could afford the satchel-size box and always took note of who was able to buy such an enormous cache of fresh-popped corn.

This popcorn experience led to taking special note of who was buying what. I noted a correlation between the size of the package and the size of the person, a connection reinforced in my consciousness by a giant, mushy thigh pushing my face against the display case as its owner made way to the counter.

The smallest-size bag had a thin cylindrical shape, bumpy on the outside from the kernels packed into it. Packed to the very top with freshly-popped corn, it had no handle and you needed to grasp the bag. It was also impossible to eat the corn in fistfuls from this size container. You had to pick the kernels out no more than a few at a time, at least until you got to the middle of the bag, and then you could dump it out into your hand. Kids purchased this one. When purchased by an adult, the adult usually looked somewhat like the bag – long and thin with bones bulging their skin like the bumps in the bag. When they ate, they would pick the popcorn out kernel by kernel and eat them one or two at a time, slowly savoring them. Most times, they would only eat half the bag and roll up the top, either throwing it away or putting it in a pocket for later.

Sears more than likely created the various size popcorn containers with consideration that one person could only eat so much popcorn. Designing the easy access top with the carrying handles, a feature for many hands reaching into the box at the same time, was probably the designers scheme for the family size, but this proved seldom to be true. The movement of shopping made it inconvenient to stop and dig into the popcorn box. In instances when more than two people were involved, a container for each was usually purchased. The size of the container was

MORE, MORE, MORE: PEOPLE NEED LESS MORE AND MORE LESS

proportional to the size of the person; small bags were purchased by small people, and big people purchased gigantic containers.

The large mushy thigh that pinned me against the counter on this particular day connected to a woman proportionally sized to the box of popcorn she was about to purchase. A mountain of flesh of such measurements I had never seen before, she was dressed in a flowered dress ballooning out over an expansive butt three times wider than I was. When you're eight years old, your head is just about the height of most adults' asses. This is uncomfortable enough, but when faced with such a preponderance of jiggling, uncontrollable flesh, it causes great panic. As I backed away, fearing inadvertently being crushed between her and the counter, I saw stocking-clad legs constricted at the knees by a roll of nylon, causing fat to droop over the stocking's top rim, and long black hairs protruding through the nylon. Caught between running away, screaming, and standing dead still until the danger passed, I backed up slowly, gazing in awe. Her arms operated awkwardly over her round, protruding belly as she tried to reach the purse slung over one shoulder. It had worked its way under her arm into a crevice. With difficulty, she retrieved it by capturing it between her massive forearm and side, and then nudging it forward. She got her purse open and took out a change purse, all of which looked inappropriately small for her hammy hands and fingers. She carefully counted out enough change, pinching each coin between a sausage-sized thumb and forefinger, and laid it on the counter.

When finished with her purchase, she shuffled away. Unable to move one foot in front of the other, she spread her feet wide apart, one moving past the other, creating dragging noises as the soles of her shoes slid across the terrazzo floor. She held the suitcase-size box perched on her belly while her hand grasped fistfuls of the fresh hot popcorn. The popcorn poked out between her fingers, and she shoveled it into her mouth, expanding her cheeks until you could see bumps on her face created by the corn stuck in there. Each fistful was rapidly replaced by another as the process continued until the popcorn had been completely devoured.

The advent of the "all you can eat" salad bar in the mid-seventies reinforced further the POPCORN THEORY OF FAT, putting a different twist to it. Fast food restaurants were taking business away from eating establishments designed for the fixed-position diner. The instant gratification of satisfying your hunger had a tremendous appeal to our ever-growing, fast-paced society. The casual satisfaction of hunger was growing in popularity. Once considered a special experience, going out for dinner was fast becoming an everyday occurrence affordable to the masses. In an effort to attract business, the sit-down restaurants invented the salad bar to allow for the expedient satisfaction of hunger. In addition, these restaurants continued to provide the more time-consuming service of the customary meal.

Restaurateurs, being good business people, realized a certain risk in offering this salad bar. It would be possible to fill up on salad without ordering the meal, defeating the purpose of increasing business and profits. The solution came in the form of plate size. Keeping the plate size small allowed a person to carry away only a certain amount of food at one time. This, coupled with the concern of people with their public image and not wanting to appear gluttonous, should have kept the situation in check. It may have worked but for the ingenuity of customers.

If you have the time to sit close to a salad bar for any period, take special note of the diners as they attack the salad bar. You will note the same behavior, taken to a greater extreme, as with the popcorn eaters. Salad, taught since we were kids, is healthy eating and low in calories. Salad must be a good thing to eat. This firmly planted in the mind, along with the "MORE IS BETTER" rule, gives rise to the mental picture of copious amounts helping rather than hindering a person.

The plate size was an impediment at first. Over time, customers developed a technique to allow for a maximum single gathering of the healthy substance. Salad building has become an art rivaling the erection of the great pyramids, with one exception. Mortar was not used in the building of the pyramids. Painstaking effort fitted each block forming the structure. This was possible because they were dealing with regular shapes and flat surfaces. This is not true in salad building. Salad building is more expansive and takes more creativity than a simple pyramid. In salad building, you contend with a myriad of irregular shapes, along with the pea problem. Peas have a bearing-type action which, if improperly placed, may cause other morsels to roll off the plate, inducing an embarrassing spill. Clearly, for salad building a mortar was mandatory.

Lucky for the salad builder, but unlucky for the restaurateur, the mortar was unwittingly provided on the salad bar. Had the restaurateurs been aware of the accessibility and the intended use of the sticky mortar-like substance, only the slickest liquids would have been provided. Salad dressings that improved building-block salad technique became their downfall. The unforeseen had happened, a tragic example of a good decision gone bad.

The building of a monumental salad is an incredible thing to witness, both in technique and agility. I will attempt to describe the technique for you in a concise manner so you will be able to identify the best in class. This will enhance your appreciation when observing a true master salad builder at work. The usual disclaimer is; **DO NOT ATTEMPT THIS WITH PAPER PLATES OR INJURY COULD RESULT**. Since the plate itself is the bedrock on which you will be building, a firm support is recommended.

The foundation is the next most important item in building a colossal salad. The foundation should be firm and well shaped to prevent shifting. Building materials are limited to the usual salad bar contents, but some of them, if carefully placed, are as solid as necessary.

In constructing the foundation, it is important not to use any salad dressing. Dressing interacts with the plate and causes a slick surface. Any tipping could inadvertently cause disaster. With that in mind, continue to build the base. Choose single pieces of lettuce, carefully turning each piece so they form a concave receptacle. As you proceed around the plate, place one piece of lettuce over the other to form an interlacing pattern. Interlocking them in this manner forms a solid skirting.

◄ THE BIG BOOK OF DAN

Next, you must find something weighty to place in the center of the cupped lettuce. Tomatoes, sliced evenly so as not to have an incline, are good in this situation; a small dollop of potato or bean salad is also a wise choice. This will form a solid base to work from, without the slickness of salad dressing. Note that the interior weight should not mound higher than the lettuce cup. This defeats the purpose and causes a weak base. Done successfully, you are able to continue without concern.

Employ fine cut carrot sticks to continue building. Being careful not to mound them, place them in a flat interwoven layer resembling Pick-up Stix when dropped at the beginning of a game. It is advisable at this point to begin mortaring together the construction with a layer of a goopy dressing, such as Blue Cheese or Ranch. The interwoven carrot sticks, with the proper amount of dressing, will simulate an adobe building material.

Another layer of lettuce, applied as the first, will form the cup shape desired to add another layer effectively. It will not be necessary to weight this layer as before because the salad dressing will act as a paste to keep it in place. Fill this cup with flat items such as sliced olives, grated cheese, or sliced tomatoes. Add a dollop of dressing, again the more goopy type, for cohesion at the center. This layer can also act as a leveling device if your salad is slightly out of kilter going into the next phase of construction.

Continue alternating layers as previously instructed as you proceed upward to the pinnacle. As you advance, be cautious not to become frivolous with the use of garbanzo beans, peas, or cherry tomatoes unless they are firmly embedded in salad dressing of a thick nature and laid in such a manner as to form a nearly flat surface. A loose cherry tomato at this point could cause a catastrophe of magnanimous proportions.

Shun the use of pine nuts or sunflower seeds at this point. They suffice as window dressing at the very end of construction. Add more of the mortar as you build. This adds flavor to the finished product, most certainly, but as it oozes out of the layers it also provides extra adhesive for odds and ends.

MORE, MORE, MORE: PEOPLE NEED LESS MORE AND MORE LESS

You may continue building in this manner, in pyramidal fashion, until you are about eight to ten inches off the base, or until your arms get tired. When you have reached the limit of your ability and stamina, it is almost time to take your salad back to your table. First, though, consider adding adornments to your creation. If you've done it properly, a dash of croutons stuck to the very top like the star on a Christmas tree is most pleasant. A swirl of alfalfa sprouts along the sides, with a dousing of sunflower seeds, will make the whole mess look like a spruce tree, specially made for your own little festive dining experience.

In both salad bars and popcorn servings, we have gone from a nation preferring small offerings to one demanding enormous portions. A twelve-ounce drink is almost unheard of when once it was the largest you could buy. The status of opulence once afforded to the rich is now the plight of blue-collar America.

What was described as an oddity in 1956 has reversed itself, as many things do with time. Being overweight is no longer an oddity but a normal and even somewhat acceptable condition. Whole industries are built on weight. First, the push was to make you fat. When the population fell more on the lean side, there was a favorable movement toward overindulging. Words like "King Size" and "Giant Size" found their way into advertising, connecting wealth and power to the ability to afford such items, and creating the impression that you were farther up the ladder of survival if you purchased and consumed the advertised commodity. As we became larger and it was ingrained throughout the media as an acceptable condition, fatness became easier and easier to sell. The advent of such marvelous inventions as fast food restaurants, where you had the opportunity to pack in as much food as you could in one day, were a blessing to mankind. They thrived.

As people expanded in girth, the connection between size and opulence became insignificant and eventually untrue. Now industries that offer the opposite state of lean and mean are flourishing. After creating entire industries to fatten you up, a new explosion in business has taken hold, the weight-loss industry. Becoming lean is the new path to survival, and the health and fitness craze has taken hold. Selling products to remove the weight that you built up from the last successful selling campaign is the new road to riches for ingenious advertizing entrepreneurs.

The snob appeal of exclusive possessing of things we have, use, or are sold seems to equate to this moving up the survival ladder theory. The popularity of the item is what makes it unpopular, with those seeking a higher position on the survival ladder. Other physical manifestations of this are seen in the cars, houses, clothes, and commodities sold every day. This outward expression of wealth, power, and exclusivity manifests in other ways, and many personal traits are recognized as being desirable.

The thing most noticeable about our behavior is its cyclical nature from one extreme to the other brought on by overcompensating for today's trends. Fat is out and thin is in. Big cars are back, small cars are out (unless the price tag is big enough to justify it being a small car). Health food is halfway in, and fat food is halfway out; pills are out, herbal supplements are in. As we grow older as a society, youth will be out and old will be in.

The only thing I can relate all of this frivolity to is what appears to be a belief that these fads and ideas lead to happiness, as if happiness is a human state that can be achieved in out-doing the next person in actions, purchasing, and consuming.

Is Reason Gone Forever?

Relieved an age of reason has past,
we can express ourselves at last.
No need to be esoteric,
expression can be more generic.

Ink, no longer reserved for print,
is liberally applied to skin as a tint.
Spider webbed elbows ensure
a clarified view of the male, mature.

Females exposed in low-slung slacks,
butt cracks punctuate tattooed backs.
I, for one, am one who yearns,
for a time of reason to make a return.

What Are We About?

On or about One Million B.C.
Australopithecine ape-man becomes extinct as the human species becomes more developed. Homo erectus erectus is unique among primates in having a high proportion of meat relative to plant foods in his diet , but like other primates he is omnivorous, a scavenger who competes with hyenas and other scavengers while eluding leopards.

꩜

Science is the only truth and it is the great lie. It knows nothing, and people think it knows everything. It is misrepresented. People think that science is electricity, automobilism, and dirigible balloons. It is something very different. It is life devouring itself. It is the sensibility transformed into intelligence. It is the need to know stifling the need to live. It is the genius of knowledge vivisecting the vital genius

Rémy de Gourmont (1858-1915)

꩜

SCIENTIFIC STUDIES OF the origins of the human state, not infer, that at one point we were scavengers fighting other scavengers for leftovers. This began with Homo erectus erectus, meaning we could walk without the use of our front legs. I am not exactly sure to what the second erectus alludes. We were somewhere down the food chain from the creatures more adept at exerting their will to survive over us lesser animals. We, according to science, were no better than those little black birds picking at flattened carcasses on the berm. Can you imagine Grandma and Grandpa hunkered down over a rotting deer carcass, taking flight just in time? Running off into the bushes to avoid being trampled by a stampeding herd of wildebeests. Well, it could have been so if at some point in time we did not change our habits. We, as individuals, must have been tired of fighting hyenas for our survival and decided to copy animals more aggressive in taking care of their needs. We must applaud the creativity in doing so, for over our brief history on the planet we have done such a good job.

Man's rapid development of the cunning necessary to compete for food with more capable creatures was a magnificent feat not duplicated by other animals; we killed all of them before they could muster the forces necessary. We, after all, were the first scavengers who banded together to become tribal hunters. The other hunters all traveled singularly or in small family packs, competing with each other for the available food. As we developed the ability to eat meat and kill herding animals, we learned to follow them. They followed their food source, vegetation. We became travelers.

Man has long been a mobile creature. He first used his feet and then animals as beasts of burden, eventually building sleds and carts to traverse land. He floated logs and created boats to travel over water. Travel allowed him to explore his world and expand his horizons.

As man began to travel across the expansive country searching for food, his awareness of other people must have grown. He certainly encountered first, a few people similar to him, then more and more similar people. The farther he went, the more he probably realized that all of these people had the same needs as he did. With a limited knowledge of the world, he most likely felt fear that the possessions needed to survive were in limited quantities. This fear no doubt gave rise to very strong emotional responses. The strongest drive of man (the animal) must have been survival, the same as with other animal species. To protect the resources ensuring survival, man had to be willing to bite, claw, kick, punch, and even kill competitors. Certainly if civilized society of today is willing to take such actions, then an uncivilized, uncultured, unlawful animal would have done as much.

The need to amass many other people undoubtedly created the

WHAT ARE WE ABOUT?

first great paradox for humankind. Realizing he was not unique, man's instinct for personal survival engendered fear. There was so much competition that this fear probably led to a paranoia concerning his possessions. How could he keep them away from others searching for the same things?

Although personal survival existed as the strongest need, man realized the safety of numbers concept from observing the behavior of pack animals. They could conquer much larger animals by their force of numbers. A conscious choice ensued: to bind with others to increase the odds of individual survival. This conscription to group living to increase the chances of individual survival is a great, unsolvable paradox.

Man's traveling proficiency allowed him the opportunity to travel farther away from his home base to find food, and it also supported expansion of the tribe without fear of starvation. With food being plentiful and mates being handy, the tribes grew larger. As the tribe grew, it soon started bumping into other tribes, and competition for food became an even more pressing issue. This led to conflict, and soon the tools used to kill animals were turned against other tribes.

Paranoia about personal survival remained the root issue. Members of the tribe recognized the necessity to protect their possessions, and the realization that safety lay in numbers led to the conscription of all.

The person who most eloquently verbalized the survival interests of the tribe probably naturally rose to incite the masses and become the tribal leader: their Adolf or Franklin or Winston. This person always ended up the prime mover. (This is why, every time we are about to blow up some country, the president, our tribal leader, makes a personal plea to each of us to join in, and he equates the whole thing somehow, no matter how loosely, with our personal survival. Whenever I hear "my fellow Americans," which is how every president I can remember has started the 'I'm going to bomb the shit out of them' speech, I go into the bathroom and vomit.)

Travel proficiency became the determining factor in man's ability to gather the necessities of living. It was also a factor in moving the weapons needed to defeat others, which in turn determined the outcome of wars he was now able to wage.

All of these factors equated to an increased ability to survive, which is a misperception. A limited amount of goods is necessary for basic survival. Once they guaranteed basic survival through gathering essentials, tribes turned their attention to gathering resources that were not necessary but might come in handy. After these articles were used for some period, they evolved into necessities. Soon basic survival was exceeded, and what became most desired was survival *in style*. The perception of what is needed to survive is similar to what is needed to make you happy: once you have that elusive article you thought necessary for survival, it goes into the survival kit. Many times, it is only a perception of something needed, and it is never actually used. Once it is in the survival kit, you defend it vigorously as a need. Now that this article is in your possession, then something else is gathered in the same manner. Soon you have all of these unused articles, perceived as necessary, for which the tribe will start wars to defend them.

This seeking of more and the subsequent development of the 'MORE IS BETTER RULE' gave us the motivation to improve transportation. This, in the natural evolution of man, became the automobile. As we met barriers to the automobile, such as oceans, the aircraft was perfected. (Then realizing that we have fouled the planet with noxious fumes from our vehicles and their byproducts and face, someday, abandoning Mother Earth, the space ship was invented.)

The increased ability to survive meant that our species could survive not only in its strongest form but also in weaker forms. Prevention of the natural culling of the species became possible. (For those unfamiliar with the culling of a species, this means that the weak, unable to survive, naturally die off, leaving the strong to breed and carry on the species). The culling process, known as survival of the fittest in all other animals, allows the gene pool to maintain a healthy status and reproduce viable, healthy offspring.

No longer did each member of the tribe need the ability to gather food or the agility and skill to hunt for it. Small groups could hunt, gather, and bring back food to the ones who could not fend for themselves. The weak, infirm, and just plain lazy could sit at home and wait for others to bring nourishment to them, which eventually led to the fast food phenomenon.

In offering the above information, I present a brief explanation for that genetic defect behind you, blowing his horn as soon as the light turns red, cutting you off on the freeway, or doing any number of things that piss you off. As any sane person would attest, the invention of mechanized transportation and its unrestricted use has created a genetic cesspool.

Survival is the main concern of every species on earth, but the survival of *other* species is left to those other species. Adaptability is the key to survival. The animals that survive will be the ones most adaptable to the environment as it goes through not only natural changes, but also those changes man has forced upon it. As we have grown stronger in our ability to kill many animals at once, in our ancient consciousness threats to humankind have unwittingly helped the scavengers grow stronger in numbers and range. The raccoon, opossum, and roach, all scavengers, are growing in numbers and ability to flourish, while the once-great predatory animals slide onto and then off the endangered species list. Would it be a great ending to our society if man is overrun and eaten by scavengers, those same scavengers from which we worked so hard to distance ourselves? I heard once on television that the cockroach could survive nuclear war; who knows, someday we may be nothing more than roach food.

At this stage of our development, we are caught in a paradox of survival of the whole versus tribalism. Transportation is at the root of the dilemma. Before transportation became the efficient system it now is, the land a tribe conveniently traveled became its boundary. Returning home within a reasonable period offered the measure of convenience. In exploring, tribes would sometimes get lost, meet up with other tribes, and form new tribes. For fear of getting lost again, a tribe might stay where it ended up and settle this new land, thus forming another tribe. As transportation expanded, this situation changed. The range of travel increased. The ability to move about became more feasible, and man could choose with whom he mingled and cohabited.

This new range erased the previous borders set by the inability to travel long distances, and it allowed one tribe to interlace with another until soon no distinct tribe was evident. This eventually led to the necessity of setting up borders to determine who owned what. Ownership of things is important; it is a measure of the ability of the tribe to survive. Survival is at the root of this whole mess.

As previously stated, the evolution of transportation also provided the evolution of man's ability to wage war. Man has never been interested in waging war for any other reason than to gain more tribal possession to ensure his survival. At the heart of any war is some dumb bastard that wants more, more, more! Having more somehow enhances survival. More guns, more planes, more tanks, more ships – all this enhances our ability to wage war, which enhances our ability to survive. This whole approach eventually led to the invention of the nuclear warhead and its proliferation to the point of having more, more, and more. Enough, in fact, to guarantee the destruction of mankind, rather than the survival of the tribal society that he started out trying to ensure.

Herein lies the paradox. As previously noted, man is only interested in personal survival. He bonds in tribes only to ensure that. Then the tribe creates boundaries to defend and invents weapons of mass destruction to carry out that defense. Mass transportation allows migration of the tribes, who then intermingle with other tribes so that no distinct tribe exists. Then tribes split into smaller tribes, allowing weapons of mass destruction to fall into the hands of just a few minor tribes. Man has provided for the certain destruction of what he was trying to guarantee in the first place, his own personal survival. It's a crazy world out there!

It is rather simple to get back to the beginning of this whole mess. It is a straight line, not figuratively but literally, *the straight line*, that was the prime cause of this whole dilemma in the first place.

The term I use for man's proclivity for the straight line is linearism.

WHAT ARE WE ABOUT?

Linearism can be directly attributed to the use of the human eye. Man did not appear on earth until long after the dinosaur was extinct. This is not to say that there were not many animals ferocious enough to make a meal out of man, but the dinosaur was not one of them. Man probably entered the food chain much closer to the bottom than his current position, spending many hours running from animals better equipped to eat him than he was to eat them. Many scientists claim that early man was an herbivore, which probably means he got the notion to eat meat from the animals that regularly dined on him.

Once man organized into packs and began using tools, he busied himself with moving up the food chain. When man got to the position of being able to either kill or drive off all predators, he believed himself to be at the top of the food chain. No other animal could claim this feat, giving man the feeling of superiority over all other animals. With time, he felt the need to separate himself from the animals, to become their master. We, as humans, have been troubled with defining why we are superior to animals since we began to feel superior to them. We have long been looking for the definitive difference between man and beast.

We need to separate ourselves from animals because we are very much like animals. We recognize at least in part that we are animals, too. However, if we are not better than animals and not separate from them, what gives us the right to herd over, butcher, and eat them? This separatism and superiority justification is still in use today, even though we have exterminated all animals that even closely threatened our existence. We have turned the philosophy of separatism and superiority on humankind in order to justify dominance over other humans.

The need to be dominant over something or someone strengthens our inner drive to feel special, which in turn makes us feel higher on the list of possible survivors. This translates from an individual feeling of dominance to a tribal feeling of dominance when we identify with a tribal group or, as we call them today, a special interest group. The special interest of a group binds it together in a common circumstance, which in some way translates to group strength and group power, making the group a definable entity and therefore a tribe, of sorts. It is why BMW drivers wave at other BMW drivers even though they do not know each other. They have a common thread, their little BMW's. It is why there is such a rush to buy team jackets. It is why there are growing numbers of street gangs and why you associate with absolute assholes that happen to belong to the same club you do.

The search for a separate identity from the animals has a very plain solution: the straight line. Man has evolved into the first linear creature. He therefore is separate from all other species on earth. Linearism, although it had a simple beginning, has been added on to and expanded until it has become an entire way of life. Linearism is based entirely on the human being and his wants, needs, and desires.

Although the straight line is abnormal and does not appear in the natural world, man began sometime in the distant past to use it and expound upon its use in his every day existence. The theory grew to explain the entire world. Straight lines represented the path for which everything came from and went back to man. It was a perception nurtured easily. Using the eye as a tool to support its existence, man saw in straight lines, so everything appeared to be within a straight line from man, and if man could not see something within the confines of a straight line, it did not exist. The effect of linearism is evident in the early popular theory that the earth was flat.

By the time man began to think straight lines were *un*natural, it was too late. Linearism had already taken hold, and there was no changing it. The acceptance of nonlinear ideas, the emotional cause-and-effect side of man's existence, was assigned a subordinate role in the common knowledge of man and his living space. You must continue to keep in mind that personal survival is the one and only important force at work here. Accepting linearism is an easy matter within the confines of one's living space. What was happening outside the personal space was of no interest to man, and if the big picture was much different than what he could see, it did not have

WHAT ARE WE ABOUT?

any bearing on his life.

As man's linear behavior became more developed, he began to use it for depicting events in his life, making cave drawings and written forms of communication. He also employed linear theory to keep track of his possessions. (The early accountants used one straight line to indicate each of the possessions each guy had in preparation for the advent of another linear notion - taxes.) From these humble beginnings, linearism became an ever-expanding tool for man.

As civilizations grew and caves were in short supply, man began to build dwellings from materials found near the settlement. These boxy structures were built in accordance with the linear philosophy, and as structures became more elaborate, it became necessary to plan them more carefully. Humans invented devices to help create these straight-line forms.

As man grew in linear proficiency, he jammed all things into his straight-line way of living. Non-linear events such as time became straight-line concepts based on the human life span. The straight line depicted everything in man's world. After all, if it wasn't in man's world, it could not exist. If he didn't see it, how could it be? Ways of calculating distances, sizes, quantities, and even the projection of time became matters of the straight-line philosophy. It was great; we had a system readily supported by all people. The eye constantly supported linearism as a mental process, the source of which was man himself. The whole idea was a marvelous invention that glorified man as the starting point and personal ruler of his linear world. The only problem is that linearism flies in the face of everything else in the universe that has been discovered since the advent of man's neat little theory of linearism. What the hell, we got something that works for us, even if it does pit us against the world. I smell another paradox.

At some point, we made a conscious decision to stick with the whole straight-line thing. Although minor attempts have been made to change the system, they have met with resistance. Linearism is the philosophy of the masses and is propagated in successive generations. It will live as long as mankind lasts. In examining the phraseology of man, linearism is in our day-to-day lives and is considered an admirable quality. In our vernacular, you will notice such phrases as: he's a straight shooter, they are on the level, the shortest way from point A to point B is a straight line, be straight with me, one plus one equals two, and what time is it. All of these are straight-line ideas and are viewed as either good or related to straight-line theories and perceptions. The straight-line philosophy is the **baseline** for the human experience. Anything outside the norm is viewed negatively, such as "he's crooked, "square pegs in round holes," or "out of square."

At the other end of the spectrum are ideas not related to straight-line philosophies and consigned to nerds and eggheads. Subjects such as philosophy are not popular with the everyday person and are looked upon as negative aspects of life, unrelated to the existence of man.

The logical thought patterns of man, which come from a most simplified portion of a very powerful computer – the human mind, give rise to the positive and negative connotations of these ideas. Society as we know it has always been stuck in one mode – the survival mode. Using the mind to feed the body is the only activity that we have consistently supported. This is evident in all of our activities, and not so much in the indulgence of these activities, but in the *over-indulgence* of these activities.

Examine more closely some of these linear ideas. How are they related to man? The first thing we need to understand is that man used only one yardstick to determine the magnitude of each part of his world. The yardstick is man himself. The size of everything in our world is measured by our size. Time is related to the longevity of the human. Numbers, quantities, physics, and natural sciences are all based on how they affect humans, therefore making the human, as perceived by the human, the most important creature on the planet and in the entire universe. These things as devised by man have one common thread: the human being's survival. Linear philosophy provides an interesting and acceptable way for the human to live, but it has spawned a perception that may not be true within the larger

WHAT ARE WE ABOUT?

realm of creation. Let's take an even closer look at the linear way we have developed and how it all works.

Consider measurements and the validity of measurements outside the world we have invented for ourselves. By measurement, we are not considering just the type of measurement done with a ruler, but rather all measurements such as size, space, quantity, weight, speed, and time. These measurements are all linear functions of numbers. Man invented these numbers and standards. To whom are all of these quantities important? To man. Do they bear any resemblance to the reality of the universe if man were not in the picture? No. These are all human devices used to define the world man perceives. Can they be wrong? Certainly not in human reasoning, because man invented them. Are they important to the rest of the universe? Probably not. Then why are they so important to man? Because they are all tools that allow man to survive in the world and communicate his separatism to other creatures, including other human beings.

The necessity to measure, quantify, and standardize the world began with the formation of tribes. Without close association of individuals, was having one as opposed to two of something important? Was the distance from here to there important? No, because how far something was just didn't matter; if you were going, you were going. Was heavy important? Not really. If it was too heavy, you didn't fool with it. If you were a singular person, not assigned to a tribe or part of a society, would anything beyond survival really matter? Would time even be an issue if you had no one to meet? Would the length of your hair be of any concern if there were no standard set? Would you be concerned with how much money you had? These are all devices to quantify, all created by man for man, with no validity outside of man. These are also all the devices keeping man from being *of* the earth and not just *on* it. They are also the devices that cause all the negative feelings within society, a society we originally created for the benefit of humankind. Are these tools, as the ultimate paradox, going to lead us to the end of mankind?

By going through this mental exercise on the development of

man, the forming of tribes, and the straight-line theory, it can be seen that the rudimentary beginnings of man in the tribal society would not have progressed without linearism. Rather than the burgeoning society of billions, man may have become extinct or at best have remained a much smaller group. But if we didn't have numbers to quantify this, it would not really matter, would it?

We can point to linearism as the one thing that separates man from beast. Without linearism, how could we possibly quantify our effect on the world? How could we count the remaining number of gorillas we have to kill before they become extinct? How could we count the casualties in our battles to determine the winner? How could we decide when to declare bankruptcy? How could we have designed and developed housing, garages, and of course that shiny new car in the garage? How could all things be as they are if we had no way of defining the way things are?

Without the straight line and thousands of years of postulates on how the world operates, it would have been impossible to conceive of the present day automobile. How could the car exist in its present form without someone putting down all of the lines that make it into a solid piece of linear mastery? What would move it along if the straight six under the hood had not been invented? How could it have been created if none of the machinery to manufacture it had been crafted? How could we have gotten along for so many years without at least one of them for each of us?

Since man created the line, he has been its prisoner. The line determines many aspects of life. There are battle lines, firing lines, bottom lines, boundary lines, lines at the bank, and lines for public restrooms, all kinds of lines for this and lines for that. First in line is important and gives you some status over everyone else in line; second is admirable but not as good as first, and so on down the line. Animals never wait in line; they're too stupid. Or are they?

Lines are the determining factor that separates us from the entire universe, holds us special, and helps us define our world, as we know it. "As we know it" is the unresolved dilemma. Is this world, as we know it, reality or just a perception created to ensure ourselves that we are actually here? Is the world we have created for ourselves a wonderful, gigantic world or a hopeless existence lived out on a speck of dust floating in some much larger creature's roll-top desk?

I felt it necessary to pontificate on humanity in this essay. I apologize if you found this boring. If you have a complaint please get in line.

Point/Counterpoint

I once had a thong
and wore it so long
that all the elastic went slack.
While others seemed edgy,
extracting a wedgie,
I found myself tucking it back.

A Dispute Over Price?

WERE WE A couple of bumpkins in town for the night or just convenient victims? I don't know why we were targeted, but it turned into one of the most outrageous and interesting episodes of my life.

Bruce, a coworker, and I traveled back to Fort Wayne, Indiana, after completing a project in Springfield, Missouri. As we approached the interchange for Interstate 65 North to Chicago, he told me he had never been there. Impulsively, I guided the car off Interstate 70 onto the ramp. We were Chicago bound. The company's home office was there, and I could always dream up an excuse for stopping in. Bruce grew more excited about our adventure as we approached town and looked forward to an overnighter in the big city.

We arrived in late afternoon. We decided to check into a hotel and go to the office in the morning. The Holiday Inn on Ohio Street had become a habit of mine since interviewing with the company. I hoped they had a room available. Fate, not luck, got us a room. As we walked through the lobby toward the desk, we had to weave around groups of well-dressed women. At the desk, a sign explained why. It read, "Welcome to the Minorities Secretary Training and Networking Seminar."

Checked in, cleaned of road film, and dressed presentably, we were off to see Chicago. Being familiar with downtown, I was the designated tour guide. Summertime and nice weather dictated our mode of exploration: we walked. Our day of travel having left us more tired than we realized, we were back at the hotel by 10:00 PM, looking for a good night's sleep.

The elevator door opened. Two small black women stood in the elevator, presumably part of the Minorities Secretary Training and Networking Seminar. We entered the elevator. I pushed the button for the 22nd floor, the doors closed, and the assault began. Instantly a hand firmly grasped my scrotum, a face came nose to nose with me, and a proposition was offered. I refused; in fending her off, the other woman accosted me. As I defended myself, Bruce did the same. It is hard to focus with your balls in the hand of a complete stranger. The skirmish lasted only to the 22nd floor. When the doors opened, the women went scurrying out and down the hall. As I adjusted myself, I felt an unfamiliar bulge in my jacket pocket. Extracting an unknown wallet, I realized we were the victims of two very skilled pickpockets. My wallet was in Bruce's pocket and his in mine, and the $300.00 from my front pants pocket had traveled off with our assailants.

I ran to the room, dialed security, and reported the incident. With thirty floors and one security guard, apprehension of the women was doubtful. Enraged, I insisted the hotel call the police so the matter could be investigated. We retreated to our rooms. As I my head hit the pillow, the phone rang. The front desk operator informed me that a police sergeant was downstairs. "Could you come down and give him a report?"

The sergeant took out a notebook and pen, leaned close in with a glint in his eye and a slight grin, asking, "Was this a dispute over price?"

A bit incensed, I said, "No, we were not drunk, not looking for hookers, and it was not a dispute over the price."

Considering Chicago's population of over six million and the insignificance of the crime, I held out no hope of an arrest. Distanced from the crime, having vented to the cop and threatened the front desk staff, I went to bed appeased. It was now midnight, and we were to be at the office at 8:00 AM. Climbing into bed, I looked forward to the few hours of rest still possible. Almost asleep, the ringing phone jangled me into consciousness.

"We caught two suspects rolling a drunk in an alley on Rush Street. They sure look like the ones you described."

My reply was a bleary "OK, now what?"

"Can you come down to the station to identify them? We can pick you up in about ten minutes." Reluctantly, I agreed to meet them in

A DISPUTE OVER PRICE?

the lobby and even more reluctantly, Bruce agreed to meet me in the lobby.

A different officer from the one who interviewed us earlier met us in the lobby to take us to the police station on State Street. He leaned close, saying, "Was this a dispute over price?"

I repeated my previous response, "No, we were not drunk, not looking for hookers, and it was not a dispute over the price."

We piled into the back seat of an offensively aromatic, beat up police cruiser with bad shocks and deafening rattles for the short trip to the State Street station. Directed inside by the officer to a stiff-backed bench in the main hallway, we were asked to wait until the detectives came in. 1:00 AM approached. Although drowsy, the parade of suspects and hope for a quick appearance of the promised detectives kept me awake. I had visions of one of these potential perpetrators grabbing a holstered handgun from a cop and opening fire on me. I viewed myself as a conspicuous target amongst the derelicts and street hustlers propped on benches against walls the full length of the hall. At about 1:45 AM, a person that appeared to be a detective approached Bruce and me. He asked us to follow him. We went down the hall, upstairs to the second floor, and into a small interview room. He introduced his partner and then leaned close to me, asking, "Was this a dispute over price?"

I peered into his eyes for a second, trying to allay my frustration, and said, "No, we were not drunk! Not looking for hookers! And it was not a dispute over the price!"

Separating us, the police interviewed Bruce and me to ensure, I surmised, that our stories matched. I don't know what they suspected. Maybe that we were two slick conmen trying to take the earnings of two poor streetwalkers through some elaborate deception. The detectives, satisfied that our stories matched, were willing to proceed. In the interview, I asked the detective what sentence a conviction would bring. He replied in a confident voice, "Oh, this is definitely a felony, and they could get up to 6 years."

Satisfied that the sentence was worth my trouble, I asked, "What's the next step?"

163

He stopped and looked at the clock, "We're going to do a lineup as soon as we round up some more usual-type suspects. It should take just a little time; it's Friday night and the action is getting heavy." It was 2:30 AM.

We sat until 3:37 AM waiting for the lineup crew to fill out. I had visions of the TV-style lineup with one-way glass and comfortable anonymity between victim and perpetrator. Finally, the time came, and everything was in place. They called me to the lineup room. I walked through the door, instantly confronted by twenty scowling, angry women. They sat in folding chairs all around me in various styles of street dress.

"Ok, pick two," said a grinning old police sergeant. You could tell what he was thinking by the look on his face: "Just a dispute over the price, I'll bet." With ease, I picked the two that had perpetrated the deed; after all, we were not drunk, we were not looking for hookers, and it was not a dispute over price.

Bruce went in next with the same outcome. Without hesitation, he picked out the two who had accosted us. The detectives had no choice but to call the prosecutor's office and involve him in the case. The process of identification took another 30 minutes or so, and by now, it approached 4:15 AM.

Shortly, a middle-aged man and a young, fresh-faced woman, both wearing business suits and carrying brief cases, walked through the office door. They set the cases down, looking at Bruce and me with solemn expressions, and the male counterpart said in a low voice, "Was this a dispute over price?"

"No, goddamn it! We were not drunk! Not looking for hookers! It was not a dispute over the price!" came my overwrought reply.

Interviewed separately, they tested our veracity again. The male lawyer took Bruce into the next room. They left me to explain to this young, virginal-looking woman how I ended up in an elevator with my testicles in the hands of two complete strangers. I stumbled through the explanation only to realize she had heard worse. Once more, we passed the test. With a bit of luck, we would not again be asked, "Was this a dispute over price?"

A DISPUTE OVER PRICE?

With Bruce and the male attorney back in the room I asked the duo, "What kind of sentence can we expect if these two are convicted?"

The male replied, "Well you have a good case; they were caught based on your description, picked from a line up."

Hesitantly, the female attorney added, "The problem is they only took cash; they can claim it was their cash, and we can't prove otherwise."

He added, "With this strong a case we can get a misdemeanor conviction; they will get six months for sure. Are you interested in pursuing the case?"

I pondered my response and decided. "Well, I guess six months would be a fitting sentence for what I have invested. Yeah, go ahead, and file the paperwork or whatever you need to do."

They conferred in private, made some phone calls, and came back into the room where we waited. Handing me a folded paper, the female attorney said, "Here is the court date and instruction on where to go, what to do. Sorry for your trouble."

We walked out the door, escorted to the same disheveled police car. I glanced at the clock, 5:35 AM.

Exhausted, we arrived back at the Holiday Inn at about 5:48 AM on a brilliant summer morning, wishing for a reprieve but knowing that the day would continue. We went to our rooms, cleaned up in preparation to meet the day, and met in the lobby for breakfast. We had not had 10 minutes sleep each. I instructed Bruce to order as big a breakfast as he could eat, and said, "Don't worry about the price." I did the same. We retrieved our bags and went to the front desk with our pre-printed bills and breakfast checks. We waited in line until the cashier became available. I presented the bills and began relating, in as loud a voice as I could muster, the tale of woe so fresh in my bleary, sleep-deprived mind. From the waiting line behind us came titters, then snickers, then raucous laughter as I recounted the events of the previous evening. The laughter and the harried voice of the cashier brought the manager in short order. With profuse apologies, he expunged our debt to calm the crowd and get us out of the lobby

◄ THE BIG BOOK OF DAN

as fast as he could. So glad that we were not having a "dispute over price," I let him off far cheaper than necessary. We went to the office, made weak excuses, and got on the road toward home as soon as possible.

The court date was set for a Tuesday morning in early September. Since I would have had to pay his salary along with all of the other expenses involved in rooms, meals, and travel, I decided to return to Chicago without Bruce. I traveled to the office on Monday under the pretense of doing some engineering work on an upcoming project. Unfortunately, I did not have the good sense to go to the hotel after work and instead went to dinner with friends. Dinner evolved into drinks, lasting far into the night. I arrived back at the Holiday Inn on Ohio Street, this time drunk, at about 2:00 AM. I got on the very same crime-scene elevator, this time alone. I awoke late with a hangover of moderate proportions. Operating on about four hours of sleep, I hurriedly showered, dressed and left for the courthouse on State Street for the anticipated date with justice.

As courthouses go, it didn't impress me. Living in Indiana, I was accustomed to majestic limestone structures with domes, ornate sculptures, and grandiose paintings depicting rural America. This dreary brick building had a factory-like appearance, dirty windows, and an institutional green interior devoid of artwork and decoration. Greeted by a uniformed police officer and a metal detector, I again felt as though I was in a potentially dangerous situation, which set my nerves on edge. Passing through the metal detector and passed over with the wand, the officer familiarized me with the seating arrangements and directed me toward the courtroom. The seats were stiff-backed, bench-like church pews. The seating arrangement, reminiscent of the bride-groom seating at a wedding, here split into plaintiffs and defendants, filling in toward the rear with family, friends, and witnesses. The room was oppressively hot, packed with people, and had the same offensive aroma as the back seat of the police car that transported Bruce and me on the fateful start to this odyssey. On the defendant's side, roped-off seating appeared to be reserved.

A DISPUTE OVER PRICE?

The proceedings began when the judge entered the courtroom and took his place behind a squat bench at the front of the room. This did not begin to resemble the Perry Mason courtroom that I had envisioned, but nothing so far had matched my mental depiction. The reserved seating soon filled with "in custody" defendants as the judge peered out between stacks of manila folders that framed his face and towered above it. The aroma of unwashed bodies ripe with perspiration, stale beer, and vomit flooded the room. Noticing the pinched noses, wrinkled faces, and gagging motions, the judge ordered the windows opened.

Viewing the defendants tempted me to look out the window to see if an anchored pirate ship flanked the curb. Among these people, I noted eye patches, missing appendages, scabs, and abundant scars. Bandanas, headbands, and hats askew topped missing teeth, gold teeth, piercings, and gaudy jewelry, which accessorized an odd assortment of mismatched and scruffy costumes. One gentleman even wore a pair of knee-high, broad-cuffed boots, unsuitable for deck wear because of the three-inch heel, but stunning with his pink mini. Looking over the pool of humanity represented by all colors, sizes, and configurations, I anticipated the coming events with trepidation, not knowing if a brawl would break out at some point in the proceedings. Surveying the lot, I noticed that the two defendants I was most interested in were not in the cordoned-off area. Scrutinizing the crowd, I finally spotted one of them in close proximity, glaring at me with hate in her eyes. My apprehension reached a new level.

With all of the players in place, the proceedings commenced with the reading of the docket. The docket consisted of the four towers of manila folders flanking the judge. The first case would not be tried for some time. I hunkered down, expecting a long process before I received the justice I sought. The reading of the docket droned on, not pausing for the El train passing under the window. The noise made it impossible to hear the court clerk, and by chance the calling of my case coincided with the clatter of the El. Had they not called it twice, my case would have been dismissed without my knowledge. I would have waited all day for a nonevent. Considering myself fortunate, I responded present and accounted for. The defendant responded angrily that she was also present. The prosecuting attorney stated, "The other defendant did not come to court and cannot be found."

Midmorning, with a break called, all but the "in custody" defendants filed into the hallways and out the doors for a cigarette and some fresh air. I returned after sucking down a couple of quick cigarettes and breathing a few deep draws of outside air. While waiting to go through the metal detector, my nemesis accosted me. She demanded an explanation as to why I so rudely pursued prosecution against her.

She asked plaintively, "Why are you doin' this to me? I just took a little of your money." I got the impression that she viewed pocket picking as her career rather than a crime. It amazed me that she had such easy access to her accuser, and I felt uneasy knowing that I was exposed to a potential assault again.

Court resumed. I sat as cases were called and charges read until about noon, at which time the docket was finished and lunch break was called.

The young female prosecutor stuffed papers in her brief case as I approached to ask, "When will my case be heard?"

"Oh, I don't know. We sure have a lot to get through. Could be today, maybe tomorrow, but certainly by Thursday."

I asked, "What do you think she will get?"

She answered, "Oh, I suppose she will get time served."

Quietly irate, I said, "What does 'time served' amount to?"

Shuffling through her papers, she replied, "Here it is, let's see, time served was two days."

"If you think I am going to stay here and pay for rooms and meals for three days to see if she gets sentenced to two days, which she has already served, you're crazy! Don't bother to go any further; I am going home!"

I retrieved my car from the pay lot for the fee of $20.00, got in, and headed back to Indiana. On my way down the Interstate, I calculated the cost of prosecution. I ball-parked the total, with a three day stay, lost time, and the initial $300.00, to be about $1200.00. Her two nights in jail would have cost $600.00 per night should I have chosen to continue the case. I surmised that, after all, it actually *was* a dispute over price.

My experience was outrageous considering the facts and interesting from the standpoint of the charges pressed. If the roles were reversed, and should I grab the crotch of a female in an elevator, I would be in prison for a long time and have to register as a sex offender for the rest of my life. No one thought to ask if I wanted to press charges other than the obvious pick-pocketing offense. Secretly, I did feel violated, but I never mention it when relating this hilarious misadventure from one summer in Chicago.

Daylight Savings Time

Ima, Litto, Teep, Ott, Short and Stout, NLC
A Paraprofessional Corporation
From the desk of
T. Cozy Esq.

April 9, 2010

Ladies and Gentlemen:

I am sending this letter on behalf of Ima, Litto, Teep, Ott, Short and Stout, NLC. I am in charge of covering this assignment as a representative of the company.

Previous correspondence concerning the matter at hand may be disregarded in favor of this communiqué. Our client, SunTrust Inc., appointed by the Federal Government under a compendium of Congressional Mandates instituted in 2007 referred to as the Unnatural Acts, has asked that we head up the team doing the Daylight Savings audit. This correspondence is necessary because of recent unfortunate events. The Unnatural Acts have now been revised to omit the words "Congressional Mandates." It seems some confusion exists over the term Congressional Mandates. Recent events have exposed some actual Congressional man dates, much to the dismay of those on the Hill. The term Congressional Mandates has been eliminated on all filing forms to remove confusion.

During a cursory inspection of accounts, the Government noticed that many citizens are in arrears and decided a general reckoning of accounts is necessary. It was decided to postpone the accounting until a census year rather than try to accomplish such a daunting task in a noncensus year.

Sun Trust Inc. is acting as the area representative of the Federal

Government under subsection 1.3 of the Unnatural Acts. Sun Trust Inc. will be the official audit coordinator of all Day Light Savings accounts for the Eastern Time Zone.

You may ask how so many citizens could be so far behind on their Daylight Savings. It is true that this is a situation not previously experienced, but there are reasonable explanations.

- Solar collectors: Many people have installed solar collectors to use sunlight during evening hours, not realizing that the sunlight collected in non-daylight savings months is directly deducted from their accounts, with interest. The hours of sunlight collected during daylight savings time and used for lighting during daylight hours are also deducted.

- Travel: Your allotted daylight is calculated based on your permanent residence. Travel to other time zones either frequently or for extended periods is the second leading cause of deductions from your account. Should you decide to travel to Alaska or the Polar Regions for extended periods, you will need to check your account balance. You may do this through Miss Conception in the Daylight Savings Department at Sun Trust Inc.

We will be scrutinizing all accounts for deficits and asking those who have negative balances to take remedial actions. Some of the remedies are listed below.

- Large account deficits: The largest account deficits will be dealt with swiftly. You will be asked to exchanges places with people living in Alaska during their extended dark period. An international exchange agreement to transport the overage to the Arctic Circle has been worked out with the Canadian government. This will also allow us to deal with the Canadian citizens who flood into the southern United States.

- Accounts with smaller deficits are of less consequence and can be dealt with through less stringent measures. Should you be found to fall into this category, you will be asked to either walk around with your eyes closed for a period commensurate with the deficit or will be given the option of standing in a dark closet for a specified time.

A grave period ahead for this country is avoidable through diligence on the part of all citizens. The dark days of World War II could have been avoided if only a little care and forethought had been exercised. In those days, daylight was rationed extensively. Many people worked nights because the shifts were longer, and they could take advantage of the small amount of daylight available. One lesson learned in those dark days was to store large quantities of daylight. The Department of Energy devised an ingenious plan from suggestions received by the constituents of Congressional Representatives. Their simple yet resourceful suggestion was to stick it where the sun doesn't shine. Congressional Representatives have received this response to other inquiries through the years but with less effective results.

The successful augmentation of this new plan will be of great benefit to all citizens. We do not want to entertain the possibility of importing large amounts of sunlight from foreign countries. The Chinese have ample amounts of sunlight, but, as seen on TV, their supply is inferior to ours. The Dark Continent, Africa, has sunlight for export. However, they will only trade for rifles and night-vision scopes. This would not be an option unless we experienced a severe shortage.

We at Ima, Litto, et al., as well as Sun Trust Inc., encourage you to participate and take seriously our audit of your accounts.

Respectfully,

T. Cozey Esq.
Ima, Litto, Teep, Ott, Short and Stout, NLC
A Paraprofessional Corporation

Life at Both Ends

THEY SQUINTED AS the dappled morning sunlight filtered through the trees. Their day had just begun, and in a most unusual way. In 1956, having any money at all was unusual, but finding money was a rare treat. Billy and Tommy had simultaneously spotted that shiny nickel nestled in the debris in the crack between curbstone and pavement. Neither could singularly lay claim to it without alienating the other. It was the rule of the neighborhood that in such a situation, money had to be split equally between them. Squatting in the street next to the curb, facing off, silent contemplation began. What was the best way to split five cents between two equally greedy young boys? As time wore on, the squat was hard to maintain. They swiveled on their heels and landed the seat of their dungarees on the curbstone, legs stretched out into the street, the silent pondering continuing, each reluctant to make the first suggestion. To start the negotiation, Tommy made the first proposal. "Let's get a Pepsi and each drink half." "We can't do that. A Pepsi is seven cents, and all we have is a nickel." Billy countered, "How about getting a Clark bar and breaking it in half?"

"Billy, that won't work. That's still six cents; there is just no way to split a nickel."

They sank back into silence.

"Billy I got it! I know what we need. We need a Tampax!"

A big-eyed Billy queried, "What the hell are we going to do with a Tampax?"

"I'm not sure how it works, but I read in my sister's magazine that if we had one of those, we could go horseback riding and swimming and even play tennis."

THE BIG BOOK OF DAN

They squinted as the morning sunlight glinted off the windows at Top's Café. Their day had just begun, and it began the same way that many have since they retired–waiting for Top's to open. Tops Café was the only place in the neighborhood that served beer with bacon and eggs, and that was how Tom and Bill preferred their breakfast.

Tom and Bill had traveled similar paths in life through marriage, child rearing, and divorce. Each now living alone, they had both been decimated by years of alimony, child support, college bills, and bad investments, and their financial prospects for the golden years were austere. Tom gazed into the back-bar mirror at their images and silently mused on how they had morphed into caricatures. Remembering those two young boys who now looked like the droopy hound and the jowly bulldog from the "dogs playing poker" tapestry hanging over the pool table, he wondered how time could be so cruel. Bill sipped on a beer and tomato juice, what he knew as a Bloody Mary, his favorite breakfast drink. He tapped the bar rail impatiently with his feet, anticipating his breakfast and hating that looking forward to breakfast was the high point of his day.

"Tom, my life sucks," Bill hissed, as John, the bartender, set Bill's breakfast in front of him.

"What is your problem, Bill? We do the same thing every day. Breakfast at Top's, sit in the park until lunch, lunch at Top's, and watch a movie on TV in the afternoon. What is wrong with that?" Tom prodded Bill with dripping sarcasm.

"That's just it–it's the same shit every day. It's paralyzing. I'm losing interest in everything. Is there nothing we can afford?" Bill's voice modulated from exasperation to desperation. "Bill, I got it! I know what we need. We need a Hoveround!"

A goggle-eyed Billy queried, "What the hell is a "hover round," and what are we going to do with it?" "Bill, I'm not sure what it is, but let me tell you how I heard about it. I got up last night at about 3:30 for my usual piss call. I sat in that lumpy old recliner, you know the one I got in the divorce, hoping to go back to sleep. The TV was on. I had almost dozed off when a voice asked, *Where are you going today?* It continued, *If you had a Hoveround, you could go to places like the Grand Canyon or the Statue of Liberty.* A different voice then said, *And it won't cost you a penny out of your pocket.* Now, I don't know what a Hoveround is, but it sounds like something we could use."

Patty Fatty and the Hunchback, Cha Cha Cha

JOSH LEANED FORWARD in his chair. *What is she doing on TV? Who would play such a cruel joke on this poor woman?*

Josh looked on nervously, waiting for her to do something. He had missed the introduction and didn't know what was happening. The judges slumped in their seats, rolling their eyes, waiting for her to begin. The camera panned the audience to capture incredulous looks. She was the most unlikely contestant imaginable. She had a moon face, thick unruly eyebrows, a nest of graying hair just barely brushed, and a bit of a mustache.

Josh thought, *She is so common and unattractive; this is not the TV norm.* He felt a pang of anxiety for the poor woman standing on stage until the first clear, unwavering note burst from her. As she continued building her song on powerful, perfect notes, he began to cry joyful tears. The judges and audience went wild with excitement and so did Josh. He danced around living room furniture, jumped over tables, and spun wildly on the rug. When she finished her song, he was exhausted from his frenzied celebration.

He knew it took courage to stand in front of that audience of tainted mentalities. Through years of media conditioning, the common perception that only attractive people have talent was obvious in the eyes of the onlookers. Josh had endured years of prejudice because of his condition. Although surgery and a cumbersome brace diminished the hump, by the time he reached middle school, he had already been labeled 'the hunchback' and it stuck. Years of offhanded rejection, smirks, nervous giggles, and name-calling caused his withdrawal into old movies and dreams.

Josh caught the program while flipping through channels. He had been watching *Swing Time* starring Fred Astaire and Ginger Rogers, airing on Turner Classic Movies. He had seen it so many times he knew most of the dialogue. Television had become Josh's refuge for many lonely years. He turned the TV off and sat in the dark, recounting the reason for all his lonely hours.

If only I had grown normally, if only my spine had developed straight and strong, if only my mom had the ability to pay for the surgeries when I was small. Well, all the "if only's" are just that, if only's. The truth is, I am what I am, like Popeye, and I had better get on with it.

Josh fell into a fitful sleep in his well-worn chair. His recurring dream again played in his mind, continuously looping from start to finish.

The club featured an Art Deco 1930's motif with a large bandstand and a large half moon dance floor surrounded by linen-covered tables. The setting replete with white and chrome décor, mirrors reflected the glimmer. The band members were dressed in white dinner jackets. They had brass, percussion, strings, a grand piano, a scintillating chanteuse, and a mustachioed lothario of a bandleader. Joshua Reynolds moved through the elegant crowd with an aplomb afforded to only the most comfortable of high society. In the customary white dinner jacket, a scarlet pocket silk jauntily tucked in his breast pocket and accompanied by a matching bow tie, he struck a grand figure. With impeccably manicured nails, a glistening pompadour, and a pencil-thin mustache, Joshua stood expectantly at the bar. His left hand rested in his jacket pocket, four fingers in, thumb out, and he held an unlit cigarette in the crook of the index finger of his right hand. A martini in a stemmed glass waited next to him on the bar. Turned toward the reveling crowd and leaning slightly against the bar with his right foot resting on the rail, he assumed the practiced pose used to attract females. This was his peacock stance, signaling availability yet aloofness that allowed for flittering on when the mood struck. It always worked for him, and soon the interplay of the nightly dance would begin.

The band launched the dancing with a foxtrot; a single lady smiled and twinkled at Joshua, a clear but subtle invitation to dance. Joshua nodded acceptance, moved to her, and escorted her to the floor. They glided around the floor to the enjoyment of the onlookers. A waltz followed, and she insisted on continuing. Joshua consented, knowing this would set the tone for the evening. He guided her by the elbow to her chair, thanked her for the dance, and took up his position at the bar. Before long, other women invited him to the floor. He floated them around with waltzes and foxtrots, seduced them with tangos, aroused them with rumbas, enflamed them with the cha-cha, and jangled them with the swing. At the end of each dance, he returned to his position at the bar to await a new partner.

Josh woke, as always, exhausted from his fitful sleep. All of the old musicals watched since childhood spawned his recurring dream. He watched *White Christmas* and *Holiday Inn* as many times as possible during the holidays and filled in the year with all of the Buzby Berkley productions he could find.

The dream did not give Josh enough of what he needed. He cleared out the basement, bought a tape player, and began practicing for two hours every night. He was not very good at first. Trying to duplicate the moves of such accomplished professionals seemed impossible. The frustration built until he found some instructional videos at the Salvation Army. He relentlessly practiced the basics, memorizing the names of each step and coordinated them with the actions until his brain could tell his muscles what to do. His muscles finally cooperated in a seamless series of moves. The tapes stressed not putting the moves to music until you could do them with confidence. In a short time, Josh was ready. At first, he only knew a waltz. The repetitious 1, 2, 3; 1, 2, 3 played as Josh focused on keeping time. He counted 1, 2, 3; 1, 2, 3, to coordinate with the constant beat of Lawrence Welk's orchestra, a tape also purchased at the Salvation Army.

He thought to himself, *If the Arabic system of counting had never been invented, dance would have a less than rhythmic appearance.* I, II, III just didn't feel the same. Josh worked strenuously to perfect his dance moves. Every evening the basement served as his ballroom, but soon the lack of a partner held him back.

So intent on practicing, Josh did not notice the onlookers kneeling at the basement windows. Chins perched on their hands, they watched intently as he danced across the floor, corrected himself, and started again. At first, there were just a few, but as word spread through the neighborhood, the audience grew larger. Soon onlookers were vying for position. Anticipating when he would start practicing, they would arrive earlier each night. The watchers were children, not familiar with the formality of dance terms. They could tell based on their inherent sense of rhythm that Josh improved with each practice.

Josh perfected his steps in the waltz and foxtrot as much as possible without a partner, and then he moved on to the Latin rhythms. He worked on the cha-cha, rumba, salsa, and tango with excitement. Having conquered his command of muscle memory, these were a little less challenging. His accomplishment of the basics in each dance allowed him now to concentrate on style. Soon his fans whispered encouragement from their perches outside the windows.

Chubby, Biscuits, Patty Fatty, and Fat Ass were all nicknames that Patty endured from second grade through high school. Fate brought Patty to the Arthur Murray Dance Studios. She was still overweight and introverted from her school-day interactions, but she needed a job and they had one. She felt comfortable with the position because it allowed her to be vivacious without being visible. Patty became the most successful phone solicitor that Arthur Murray Studios ever had.

Patty finished her list of leads each night in record time. She always managed to charm two or three people into taking the introductory package at $125. When finished, she watched the dance instructors and students through the one-way mirror. The instructors used the mirror to observe students, picking out the most enthusiastic ones to later approach with the full package of lessons. As much as Patty enjoyed watching, she longed to be out on the floor even more. Her size and shyness kept her in the back room, offering strangers what she secretly wanted for herself. The desire to dance set Patty's will to lose weight in motion. She attacked weight loss with a determination forged by the desire to be that lithe image floating across the floor.

As she lost weight, she noticed heads turning as she departed. At first, there were just a few, but soon all of them swiveled to follow her from the office door to the front door. She felt the piercing envious stares of the female students and the longing lecherous gazes of the men..Patty went from the unnoticed, fat girl leaving the studio each night to the mysterious, hot chick asked about by all the male students. She took delight in the newfound attention. Because of all the inquisitive male students, and as a reward, management offered Patty a beginner series of lessons at no cost. Patty attacked dance with the same determination as weight loss. She graduated from beginner to the next level and soon danced competently with the instructors.

Friday night was dance night at the studio, and she became the most sought-after female noted by the vocally demonstrative dismay of the female students. Male students lined up to dance with her.

The annual Show Case planned for October rapidly approached. It featured a friendly student competition, dance party, and dinner. Patty both anticipated and dreaded the event. She wanted to show off her new skills but had no regular partner. Her interaction with the male students was unrewarding. They were all more introverted than Patty Fatty had been. Their dancing was stiff and amateur, their conversation awkward. The male teachers spread themselves around to satisfy all the ladies, and Patty had advanced well past dancing with other women. She wanted to bust out and show her stuff, but she did not have a capable partner.

♪♪♪

Charlie, come back here!" Patty shouted after her brother. Charlie, her six-year-old brother, was heading out the backdoor. "Where do you think you're going?"

"Patty, I have to go or I'll miss my spot."

"You're not going anywhere until you eat your dinner! Mom asked me to watch you until she gets home, and the first thing I'm going to watch is you eat dinner. Now sit down!"

THE BIG BOOK OF DAN

Charlie sat at the kitchen table and feverishly shoveled mashed potatoes and corn into his mouth. Then he grabbed a pork chop, sank his teeth into it, ripped a chunk off, and gulped that down.

"Charlie, slow down! You're going to choke to death. What is your hurry?"

Charlie gasped between gulps, "I'm going to lose my spot!"

"Your spot for what, Charlie?"

"The show. There, I ate. Now can I go?"

Exasperated, Patty asked, "*What* show, Charlie?"

"I'm late. I gotta go!"

"Sit down, Charlie. You are not going anywhere until you tell me what this is about."

"Okay Sis, but listen fast because I gotta go. You know the hunchback, Patty?"

"Charlie, his name is Josh, and yes I know him. I went to school with him."

"Well, every night about this time he goes into his basement, plays this weird music, and whirls around the floor."

"What kind of music, Charlie?"

"Sometimes like the stuff Grandma listens to, but sometimes it's like the stuff the gardener plays. Now can I go?"

"Yes you may, but I am going with you."

Patty followed Charlie to Josh's house. She was stunned to see three or four children at each of the basement windows. They were squished together, kneeling with their butts up and their chins resting on their hands as they peered into the windows. Charlie strong-armed his way into one group of three. Patty stood back, not wanting to be pushy. When she could not stand it any longer, she horned her way in, displacing two disgruntled little girls.

She silently thought, *You girls are lucky; last year there would have been no room for anyone but me.* Patty had an inkling of what Charlie had described, but when she saw Josh dancing around the basement, she was amazed. Elegant and poised, he had great rhythm and impeccable posture. She watched for some time. Suddenly feeling like a trespasser, she retreated to her mom's house with Charlie in tow.

Patty began plotting a strategy to lure Josh to the Arthur Murray Showcase. She knew that he was the partner she needed to show off her talent. She also knew that the plan would need to appeal to him enough to drag him out of his comfortable hiding place. She decided to compose a special invitation to the upcoming Showcase. She labored over the language until it all jumbled together and nothing sounded adequate. She finally decided a seemingly heartfelt, simple explanation would be the best.

Dear Mr. Reynolds,

If you were to look out your basement window as you practice, you would see your entourage softly cheering your every move. They have great confidence in your ability. They have brought your efforts to the attention of one of our instructors. We are always looking for new talent to teach and compete. We would like to invite you to our annual Arthur Murray Talent Showcase as a special guest. It will be this October 23rd at the Sheraton Inn. Formal attire is required. Please RSVP as soon as possible.

Sincerely,
David Valentine

Patty put her home address on the RSVP card. She did not tell Mr. Valentine about the letter and hoped it would not come up. She felt the intrigue would be worth a reprimand if Josh did show up.

Josh received the letter in the mail, puzzled over the stationary for a moment, and then opened it. He sat in his recliner in front of the TV. Looking first at the letter, then at the TV, and then back again, he pondered what he should do. He had spent all this time practicing; maybe he should try it, then again, maybe not.

I want to, no, I don't, yes I should, then again, maybe not. His old haunting thoughts came back. *If only I had grown normally, if only my spine had developed straight and strong, if only my mom had the ability to pay for the surgeries when I was small. Well, all the "if only's" are just that, if only's.* Luckily, truth came with them. *The truth is, I am what I am, like Popeye, and I had better get on with it.* Damn right I'm going.

Josh decided if this were to be done, it would be done right. He went to a first-class hair stylist, hoping George, his regular barber, would never find out. He had his nails manicured. Next, he made an excursion to a first class tailor. He picked out a dinner jacket and trousers of a quality cut. The tailor altered the sleeves to allow for his slight irregularity, so that the sleeves of the jacket and shirt cuffs landed exactly right at the wrist of each hand. Josh also selected a fashionable scarlet bow tie and matching pocket silk. He found a pair of black ostrich dress slip-ons that gripped his foot comfortably without slipping. He even bought first-class underwear. He thought, *If nothing else, good underwear always makes you feel dressed.*

When the RSVP card arrived in Patty's mailbox, she almost fainted. After recouping her composure, she began to plan. She had intended to wear an unflattering, straight-cut sheath and a sweater to fend off the usual dance studio haunts, but with Joshua's acceptance, new strategies needed formulation.

Patty visited the most prestigious salon in town to get a facial, a manicure, a pedicure, and a new hairstyle. She also made an appointment to have her makeup done the evening of the dance.

At her next stop, she purchased a beautiful, shimmering, black cocktail dress with spaghetti straps, reminiscent of an Audrey Hepburn style. She insisted a tailor look at it to make sure the fit was absolutely perfect.

The evening of October 23 was filled with apprehension for Josh and anticipation for Patty. The ballroom featured an Art Deco 1930's motif with a large bandstand and a large half moon dance floor surrounded by linen-covered tables. The setting replete with white and chrome décor, mirrors reflected the glimmer. The band members were dressed in white dinner jackets. They had brass, percussion, strings, a grand piano, a beautiful female vocalist, and a mustachioed lothario of a bandleader. Joshua Reynolds moved through the elegant crowd with an aplomb afforded to only the most comfortable of high society. In a white dinner jacket, a scarlet pocket silk jauntily tucked in his breast pocket and accompanied by a matching bow tie, he struck a grand figure. Joshua, groomed impeccably with manicured nails, a glistening pompadour, and a pencil-thin mustache, stood expectantly at the bar. His left hand rested in his jacket pocket, four fingers in, thumb out, an unlit cigarette held in the crook of the index finger of his right hand, and a martini in a stemmed glass waiting on the bar. Turned toward the reveling crowd, leaning slightly against the bar with his right foot resting on the rail, he held a practiced pose.

He turned to see a woman of incredible beauty. She had black tresses cascading over creamy Irish skin and a long, elegant neck descending to a lithe, slender body. Her appearance captured his imagination, his dreams, and his heart. She turned to pose in profile, put her back to him, and then turned to present her opposite, perfect view. When she turned to face him, piercing emerald eyes met his. She smiled, demure, and sealed his fate.

The band began with a foxtrot; she twinkled at Joshua, a clear but subtle invitation to dance. Joshua nodded acceptance, moved to her, and escorted her to the floor. They glided around the floor to the enjoyment of the onlookers. A waltz followed, and she insisted on continuing. Joshua consented, hoping this would set the tone for the evening. He led her back to her chair, thanked her for the dance, and took up his position at the bar. He turned to look at her and knew then that there was nowhere else to be.

He floated her around with waltzes, then foxtrots, seduced her with a tango, aroused her with a rumba, enflamed her with a cha-cha, and jangled her with a swing, all the while reveling in the blossoming of his dear friend who suffered the torment of not growing up like everyone else. Circumstance and chemistry bonded them, evermore.

Philandering

I do believe explicably,
that the opinion expressed predictably,
would be eased intrinsically,
if the deed were done explicitly
for those most in need statistically.

Perhaps the feeling needs expressing
that the outcome you should be addressing
for those most in need of a sexing,
is that philanthropic philandering
would appear much less like pandering
if the need is what you are stressing.

It is easy to be desirous
of young, lithe creatures that inspire us,
but for the view to be given weight
you must fully be willing to date
those broad of beam or on a stretcher.
If not, you're just a typical lecher.

Bubba and Me

WAITING TO USE the pay phone in the town square, I looked down in time to dodge a stream of urine rolling down the sidewalk from under the phone booth door, a less than propitious introduction to Leesburg, Louisiana, and a precursor of an epigrammatic yet excruciating period of my then young life.

In June of 1969, one thing coveted above all else by my acquaintances and me, all marooned in Leesburg, Louisiana, was a way out of Leesburg, Louisiana.

Fort Polk, combined with Leesburg, was the pit of the universe. Days and nights were sweltering hot. The barracks were old, dusty tinderboxes without air conditioning. Built as a segregated fort during WWII, eleven miles separated the section constructed to house white soldiers from the section built for black soldiers. Our barracks were on the side originally built for the black soldiers. Scarce amenities were obvious in our billet area. Hospital facilities, the main PX, and a comfortable air-conditioned movie theater all lay eleven miles down the road.

Leesburg, a scruffy little town, the watering hole for every soldier in the fort, looked worn and weary. The main street, a series of bars, arcades, pool halls, and pawnshops, devoid of civilians except for proprietors, catered to the military foot traffic staggering in and out of each establishment looking for somewhere to drink, something to do, or a place to trade a class ring for cash. Foot traffic in Leesburg swayed with a rhythmic, alcoholic swagger, replicating passengers on a cruise ship in heavy seas.

I waited with growing anticipation for discharge and escape. Billeted with a holdover group, we looked forward to mustering out of the army.

Army restrictions and supervision eased because we were on

our way out and the management did not want to waste time on us. However, they did want to make sure we did not sit idle waiting for discharge. Sergeant Johnson organized work details every morning after reveille. He was desperate to find work for me. I had a doctor's excuse that got me out of most work. After studying my excuse, he found KP to be the only duty that I could perform. Kitchen duty was my permanent assignment for the duration. Bubba suffered the same fate, and that is where we met.

Bubba had been Bubba all his life. He had no concept of the term's derogatory connotation. Eight inches taller than my 5 feet 11, he was well muscled from working his father's shrimp boat from the age of seven, and at about 250 pounds, he dwarfed my 180. He walked with a rolling gait as though taught to walk on a shrimp boat chugging through the rollers. Cajun by birth and nature, he could be an ardent friend or a fierce enemy depending on your treatment of him. Fortunately, we became great friends.

The barracks were familiar to me; I had just spent eight weeks living there as a truck driver trainee. Bubba transferred from an infantry company. Other members of our group of misfits came from companies all over the fort, the hospital psych ward, and the stockade. The assortment of personalities and backgrounds made for an interesting band of oddballs.

Bubba and I, being on perpetual KP, woke every morning at 4:30. We reported to the assistant cook, Leonard Chuckles PFC, for duty. Leonard was Bubba's height but spindly and gaunt looking in his cook's whites. A drawn face with rosaceous cheeks and a nose rivaling that of W.C. Fields complemented his watery, blood-laced eyes. He was a charming soul who, after 11 years in the army, attained Private First Class. He had risen to the rank of Staff Sergeant several times, but an errant lifestyle and a small drinking habit always plunged him back down again. This made him a less than pleasant person, and he did not hesitate in taking it out on us. Between his bitching from the kitchen and the smart remarks from the chow line, it was a trying time every day. Cooking and serving breakfast, we endured a barrage of remarks about the quality of the food. When asked, "How do you want your eggs?" the common retort was, "Why don't you stick your dick in 'em, you're going to fuck 'em up anyway." It got old fast. Bubba told me that the over-easy eggs always made a sizzling sound if you spit on them before you flipped them. We just grinned and slopped food on their plates, those unsuspecting bastards. You should never piss off the kitchen help. It is unsanitary.

After 4:30 a.m. starts and 8:00 p.m. finishes, it was all we could do to drag over to the PX across the street, choke down six Falstaffs, and flop into bed. Next morning it started all over again, a recurring nightmare from Monday morning to Saturday morning. Saturday, after breakfast cleanup was complete, we were free. We rushed over to the barracks, showered, put on civvies and got a taxi to Leesburg. Once there, we realized we didn't want to be there, but the need to break the monotony of barracks life drove us to it.

Catching a bus to Lake Charles was too expensive for such a short time. Leesburg was our only option. The self respecting southern girls vacated town after the fort was reactivated for training during the Viet Nam War; only tattered old barmaids, thickly crusted, ornery, and not well versed in conversational English, remained. When your ass hit the barstool, "What the hell do you want?" served as both a greeting and a question. You had better bark out the answer as though she were a boot camp drill instructor, or you didn't get served until she was ready to ask again. The bars had so much foot traffic that the urinals constantly ran over, and there was an overriding odor of vomit. It was so bad that if you needed to empty a few out, you might as well just stand up and piss on your shoes. After a few trips to Leesburg, the essence of stale urine wafted up from your leather soles scorching on the hot pavement. Bubba and I would drink a few beers and then retreat before they hit bottom and were ready for expulsion.

We pushed our way past the ever present throng of drunken boot camp trainees, staggering around town looking for the nonexistent female population. Three blocks off the main street, one could find a greasy spoon with acceptable food but few customers. The bathrooms were passable. A curious sign, "We grind our hamburger fresh daily," hung over the door. Army food was not the best; you would think there would be a line at the door to get a good hamburger. It puzzled us why half of the stools were empty until we saw the cook. His cook's whites were an unsavory shade of grey, his hat had a sweat ring darkened with age, and crusty bloodstains splotched his apron. On his left hand all that remained were a thumb and a pinky finger, on the right a thumb and index finger. He chewed on a cigar stub and coughed incessantly. To think he ground the hamburger daily could cause most to beat a hasty retreat.

The pie was good, the coffee acceptable, the urinal flushed, and the floor was dry. Compared to most of the bars, this was a four-star establishment. However, its charms wore thin after a few visits.

Bubba and I were sitting at an ass-polished, splintery picnic table at the PX splitting a six-pack of Falstaff. In the heat, trying to race to the end of three without the last swallow being intolerably tepid was a challenge. As we drank, we began discussing our favorite topic, Leesburg. As always, we decided that we would not go back. As we sat complaining about all of our bad experiences, PFC Chuckles exited the PX with a six-pack of Pearl under each arm and walked purposefully toward our table. To our surprise, he sat down with us. A terse and decidedly unfriendly attitude in the kitchen had not led us to suppose he would be at all friendly outside that environment.

PFC Chuckles sat listening to our droning on about the evils of town as he struggled to loosen the grip of the plastic retainer constricting the containers of Pearl, hampering his quest to quench a thirst and escape his reality. The first can fizzed and spit when he popped the top, a result of all the jostling during the initial struggle to free his prize from the plastic restraint. He put his mouth around the opening to capture the gurgling liquid, minimizing loss of his desired medication. He hurriedly tipped the can, Adam's apple pumping up and down, as he greedily consumed the entire first can. Dribbles dripped from the corners of his mouth and found purchase on his bloodstained cook's white shirt. His belly was a half-round protrusion peculiar to his scrawny, meatless frame; a catchall for everything that gravity caused to pass by his chin, a belly giving the appearance that he was smuggling mixing bowls from the kitchen. Bubba and I attributed his appearance to premature liver failure.

He sat and listened to our ruminations until he had gulped down his third beer. Popping the top on number four, he turned to us and said, "How long have you assholes been here?"

Looking inquisitively at him, I could not believe he spoke to us. He had never spoken a civil word to us, and even work-related communication consisted of snorts, gestures, curses, and clipped instructions.

"Well, how long have you assholes been here?" He repeated, in an exasperated timbre.

"I can't speak for Bubba. I've been here 3 months and 10 days and hope to be gone soon."

He retorted, "You mean in 3 months and 10 days you have not reconnoitered the attractions and finer points of beauty in the city of Leesburg, Louisiana?" With a bemused snicker he queried, "What kind of lame-ass soldier are you? It took me little time to find the premier drinkin' spot in this dump."

I thought if anyone could find a good bar in this town it would be PFC Leonard Chuckles. To qualify his veracity, I asked gingerly, "Were you drunk or sober when you found this wonderful place?"

Grinning like an exultant child he said," I was sober when I found it, drunk and satisfied when I left."

"Okay Chuckles, let us in on your discovery." Bubba said with a twinge of skepticism

Chuckles drew close to us, and whispered, "Promise not to spread it around; we don't want the place overrun with drunken', puke stinkin' E-1's."

"All right Leonard, we promise." We said in unison. I was feeling like a third grader at a secret club meeting; Bubba probably felt the same.

Leonard drew even closer and mumbled, "The next time you are in town, find a cab, ask the driver to take you to heaven, he'll know what you want." Chuckles let out a raucous, evil laugh, picked up his remaining beer, and tottered toward his barracks.

Incredulous, Bubba queried, "Now what the fuck does that mean?"

"I don't know Bubba, but it may just be worth a try. I'm willin'," I said, as we adjourned for the night, full of beer and curiosity.

If those shiny, spacious new cars of the Fifties and Sixties could be called land yachts, by the time cab drivers put them into service, ferrying soldiers around town, they were tramp steamers. Large, well-worn vehicles clunking and rattling, pitching and yawing around the corners and down the streets delivered the deluge of revelers to their favorite haunts. We were about to flag one down to transport us to Leonard Chuckles' favorite refuge, a place he referred to as heaven.

The circumstances leading up to our decision undoubtedly culminated in our eventual dilemma.

Our interest peaked during the week after that fateful night outside the PX. We doggedly pursued Leonard all week, asking at every opportunity for more information. He grinned; reiterating his original comment, "Take a taxi ride to heaven." Breaking into his evil laugh, his next comment was, "Get your lazy asses back to work." The lack of information combined with the malevolent laughing lent to our anxiety but also a gnawing curiosity. We were going, for sure, but armed with enough liquid courage to stave off jitters brought on by our trepidation.

Saturday evening was spent in the public park. We bought a bottle of Myers dark rum, a libation outside the realm of our usual beer menu, something we had not tasted. The first drink burned all the way down and continued to smolder in the stomach. We could not drink more as it was but could not squander our investment; we diluted it with water to the point of tolerability and drank on. (Some years later,

I found out that rum diluted with water was a common seafarer's drink called grog.) Continuing drinking through the evening, we became stinking with courage, enough so that we hailed a cab to take us to Leonard Chuckles' heaven.

A brutish looking '59 Pontiac squealed to a rest in front of us, I opened the door to a cloud of smoke drifting out and a gruff "Get in before I lose my cool air." Over-sized air conditioners, the only consistent feature and a necessity in the sub-tropical climate, cooled taxis to bone chilling temperatures. We hurriedly piled in, slammed the door, announced to the driver that we wanted a ride to heaven, and slouched back on the tatty, stained seat. The repugnant laugh from the front seat made me spring forward. For a brief, horrifying instant, I thought Leonard had a part time job.

Relieved that the driver only sounded like Leonard, I settled into my seat, lit my cigarette to contribute to the ambiance, and waited for a response. The laugh, a little longer this time, preceded a brief reply, "I know what you boys want. Hold on, we are on our way."

As we drove in silence, I nervously gawked, taking in all the details of driver and cab. If dumped in the middle of nowhere, I wanted to be able to give a reasonable, albeit alcohol-skewed, description of the perpetrator. Our driver peered at us through a rearview mirror accented with large, pink, fuzzy dice, black dots peeling off undoubtedly as a result of the toxic exhaust vapors billowing up through the floorboards. A creased, weary face looked back at me, the thin-lipped sneer holding a burning cigarette. His face radiated orange with each deep draw, further accentuating the furrows in his countenance. At the exhale, the glow of the speedometer backlit the escaping smoke with an eerie green as it drifted up to the ceiling. Cooled by the chill of the air conditioner and blown toward us, we sat in a bank of dank smoke like a hovering fog.

A fringe, pinned to the head-liner at the windshield, rippled with each turn and bump as the behemoth lumbered down the asphalt on bald tires and age-weakened shocks. The lights of Leesburg receded in the rear window as we drove. This would have been worrisome had we not seen lights rising in front of us. Suddenly a momentary feeling of weightlessness, the fringe jumped and fell in unison, and the unmistakable sound of rock crunching under tire and pinging on the floor confirmed the end of the paved road. The look on my face must have been a clear indicator of alarm.

The driver mused, "Well boys, heaven is just around the next turn."

We saw a blue hue through the sparse stand of trees, and as we turned that last corner, a long, single-story, block building stood in the clearing. Large blue, neon letters mounted on the front of the building announced **"Heaven"** and confirmed our arrival. The big old Pontiac eased into a space, pulling close to the barrier pilings before coming to rest. Our driver exacted his toll of $10.00, backed slowly out into open space, gunned the engine, dropped into gear, and sped off into the night, leaving a wake of flying stone and dust.

We stood in the sign's luminous blue cast at the large double industrial doors, each with a handle in hand, about to pull open the entrance to what Leonard said would be heaven. As we began to pull, the doors swung open effortlessly. A man in a snowy white suit, his size rivaling Bubba's, greeted us jovially and beckoned us to enter. The contrast of the man's dark skin and pure white suit was transfixing. As we looked around and drank in the atmosphere, it was clear that we were "not in Kansas" anymore.

Far from the sleazy bars of Leesburg, in distance and comparison, Heaven seemed aptly named to the soldier experienced in the Leesburg bar scene. The floors of polished, industrial-grade tile rivaled any barracks; walls painted in bright colors and covered with sports posters lent to the masculine atmosphere. Pool tables with flawless greens busied by appreciative aficionados stood to one side. A welcoming cluster of four-top tables occupied equal space on the other side of the room. A long bar with bar stools anchored to the floor stretched across the full length of the room, spaced to give elbow-room to even the largest of patrons. A jukebox provided music from rock to soul to whet the tastes of most, and a dance area next to it provided an added diversion. Having an immediate need, I found the men's room first thing. Gleaming porcelain, sparkling stainless steel, and the unmistakable aroma of Clorox greeted me. Back out in the barroom, to best all of the wonderful attributes of Heaven, the place overflowed with angels, angels in cocktail dresses, well groomed, perfumed, made up, and smiling. They ranged from intriguing sepia to deep chocolate, each a temptress of beguiling virtues, especially to a liquor-swilling, companion-starved, soldier who has lived in an all-male environment for the last six months.

Bubba and I wandered around, mesmerized by this oasis of pleasure. The Myers rum had not worn off, but we were ready for more. For some reason Tequila was chosen as the appropriate beverage to celebrate our good fortune. Fortunately, for our budget, management believed in pouring stout drinks in large glasses. It did not take long to get back to and then surpass our previous level of intoxication. Our liquid cash was rapidly turning into actual liquid; we needed to make an approach while we still had something to offer. Eyeing the women sitting at the tables, seductively beckoning with smiles and winks, we soon picked out two who attracted us.

Bubba's choice, a dusky woman with a bright smile framed in vivid red lipstick, sat cross-legged, an arm draped over her chair back. He walked over and she stood to greet him, just a half head shorter than he. She filled a scarlet, strapless dress with a more than bountiful figure. Animated in mannerism, even boisterous, she overtook him immediately. Within minutes, they disappeared out a door next to the bar.

A beautiful woman, the hue of creamed coffee, walked by my table. A salty, spiced aroma wafted from her as she passed, and I fell into lockstep behind her. My attraction, magnified by stimulants, was palpable. She turned to penetrate me with sparkling, lime-green eyes probing the depth of my attraction. At that moment, a suggestion proffered and a proposition made met a willing ear. I followed her out the same door that, moments before, Bubba had exited with the woman in the red dress.

The door opened to a rutted, well-worn path leading to a small motel adjacent to Heaven. Years of use, obvious by threadbare carpet and peeling, outdated wallpaper, exposed the seedy reality of what Leonard touted as heaven.

Sobering quickly as we reached her room, I became first hesitant, then belligerent, wanting nothing more than to get the hell out of there. As I began to refuse, she realized that the trip would be for nothing and a loss of revenue was imminent. She rushed to a bureau, opened the drawer and, pulled out a serrated, plastic handled steak knife. She brandished it in my direction and with a shrewish, hissing voice, she said, "If this don't get it I got a gun, too." Those once attractive eyes turned to hate-filled slits, the comely smile to a tempestuous sneer.

Running out the door, throwing the last of my money over my shoulder, I yelled, "No, that'll do!"

Meeting Bubba on the path, we decided it was time to retreat. Although his experience seemed to be satisfying to him, the results were the same; we were both stone-broke and miles from Leesburg, and farther still from Fort Polk. Walking over the stones in the middle of the night, we resolved to stay in hell rather than risk another trip to PFC Leonard Chuckles' Heaven.

I spent Sunday nursing a painful hangover and swearing the hangover pledge: "I will never drink that much again." Monday brought my prayed-for paperwork. Ordered to Headquarters, receiving my last pay, and released from duty, I rushed to turn in my gear. I caught one of those behemoth taxis to Leesburg and then a Greyhound to New Orleans. The bus driver dropped me at the New Orleans Airport, and soon I arrived safely in home port, relieved that my odyssey was over.

Getting Old

Age and Aging
I don't believe one grows older. I think that what happens early on in life is that at a certain age one stands still and stagnates.

>T. S. Eliot (1888-1965), Anglo-American poet, critic.

Old Age
The tragedy of old age is not that one is old, but that one is young.

>Oscar Wilde (1854-1900), Anglo-Irish playwright, author.

I AM FORTY-NINE years old in linear terms. Forty-nine is a precarious age. I am too old to chase young women and too young to chase old women, not that I want to chase old women. The good thing about the linear concept of time and statistics is that the older you get, the more young women there are. The bad thing is that age as defined by the passing of time is not a concept readily accepted by the mind.

I saw, read, or heard that the mind has a way of not letting you smell yourself. The person talking about this said it was part of your defense mechanism. This I believe to be true. Shortly after you put on after-shave, you cannot smell it, but those around you can. This is a curious attribute to have, but I think it goes deeper than just being able to smell yourself. I also believe that the mind, as part of this same mechanism, doesn't let you really see yourself. I think for most of your life you remain fixed at a physical age, only in your mind, but it is how you perceive yourself for many years. I don't know when you get the full realization of your true age, or even if you ever do, because I haven't gotten there yet.

I shave this face every morning, I look at it carefully, I check it for cuts, bruises, abrasions, pimples, and blemishes, comb the hair above it and finally pull a shirt over it. After dressing, I look at it again before sending it out into the world to a new day. After walking away from the mirror, I promptly detach myself from it and have no mental concept of what it looks like. I have no conscious thought of this face all day and, should I happen to glance in a mirror, I am shocked by how old it looks. It is I. On some mental level, I know it is I, but on the very surface of my mind it is not. This may sound strange. I have never heard anyone talk about this. Maybe it is such a subtle concept that people don't notice when they also experience this. Maybe they do and don't talk about it for fear that not everyone experiences it, and they might be thought of as crazy.

My picture of me is certainly not that guy I shave every morning. I am younger and taller and thinner than he is. He is just some guy that needs grooming, and I am the only one around to do it for him. I think everyone's personal mental picture is much more flattering than what he looks like, but what do we actually look like? I know what I think I look like, I know what I feel like, and it isn't that guy I shave in the morning. If you can't smell yourself and you can't see yourself, are you really there? Of course you're really there, you can touch yourself, can't you? So, you are really there. It's just that you are someone else. Get it?

From the time I walk away from the mirror until the time I walk in front of another, which I try to avoid, I am Zorro. I am tall, thin, extremely handsome, ageless, and very elegant. I can't figure out why the young women I flirt with don't fall all over themselves. This Zorro thing is not a conscious portrayal (I don't wear a cape and carry a sword) but an example of how I perceive this character that goes out into the world every day. I don't, in my surface mentality, see the old fart I have become; all of the scars of living I gained over those hard-lived forty-nine years are mysteriously absent. From time to time I

GETTING OLD

look at others, pondering how old they look, how old they must feel, only to find out that they are younger than I am. It is a small jolt of reality to think of someone as old and then find out that he is younger than you are. It is one of those little jolts that momentarily bring you to reality, similar to the noise of the barber's shears too close to your ear. Yes, you can hear the shears, but you tell yourself it is nothing more than a closer-than-usual trim of the sideburn. Then you feel the tickle on your ear and know it is the dreaded trimming of the ear hair that he is performing, a definite sign of old age, another little jolt of reality.

All of these little signs persistently nag at you but are pushed out, ignored, and denied. The denial goes on past forty-nine. At forty-nine, I am still eighteen for most of my day. How much past forty-nine does this denial go? It scares me to think about it. When does it end? Who knows? Certainly in previous generations it must have not been so. My grandmother was perpetually old. I can never remember her being anything but old. My parents were not always old but were old for a longer period of time than I plan to be. When did old become a dirty word? When did middle age become something that at forty-nine I don't believe I am yet? When did youth become something we want? I believe it all happened in our generation, baby boomers, as we are called. Why did it happen? It is not our numbers, earning power, or various other factors pointed out about this group of post-war babies that makes us special in our quest for youth. It is something that was non-existent to previous generations.

The one and only culprit to blame for our penchant for youth and staying young is the television set or what has become known as the TV. (I believe it was given the initials "TV" to make it sound more like a friend than an appliance.) I believe the acceptance of the TV into our lives has done more to create an insatiable quest for youth than any previous gadget. The TV allows us to remain suspended in a time warp of nostalgia in the programs it offers, and it sells products to keep you seated and attentive during regular interruptions called commercials. These insidious one-minute periods offer every remedy imaginable to keep us young, healthy, and fit to live past all previous statistical longevity predictions.

It is difficult to get a grasp on time and the ages of those around you. When some star of past years dies, the newscaster reporting the story says this person that you saw just the night before died at eighty-something. Momentarily, you are caught thinking how young they looked in that movie last night, only to realize that the movie was made in 1943. It is this miracle of the suspension of time that gives a false sense of agelessness. The mind creates a reality for you from years of training; your mind fills in the blanks between what is actually real and your vision of what is real. This is similar to looking from some distance at a painting.

When you look at a painting from a distance, your mind will tell you what is there even if it isn't. You may see faces in a painting of a crowd. You will see eyes and mouths. You will see expressions on those faces. When you get closer, you only see blobs of paint that don't resemble any of the features your mind told you were there.

The mind also tells you that your reality is based on recalled past experiences. The television presents the mind with images of life that are not real and have no reference to time or the actual physical world around us. If you allow your brain to accept all of these images without other references, it could believe that these television images are reality. We were fortunate, people my age, because our television watching didn't start until we had established the difference between the real world outside our houses and the unreal world brought to us through that box. I was nine years old when we got our first Philco, and at that time there were only a few programs on TV to watch. Our social code and morality were already established by the time we became TV watchers. The children of today are set in front of the box so early that they are learning their moral code from the TV. Exposed to unreality so early, it becomes their reality.

Even though our reality was established at a very young age, and we can differentiate between reality and fiction, we still get caught up in television's propaganda. This insidious propaganda flies at us so rapidly and so often, we become brainwashed, believing many of those images and sound bytes are actually true. This is the motivation behind all of those interruptions in programming called commercials. Commercials are the chosen way of programming each of us to act upon everything, from what detergent to buy to whom to vote for in the upcoming election. They have become such powerful tools that our presidential hopefuls use them, instead of full-length programs, to sway us to vote for them. They have come to realize that we will choose our regular programs over any debate or half-hour monologue on their aspirations, so they stuff themselves into those one-minute spots to tell us all about themselves. We have become a country ready to accept a president on fifteen minutes of information that we heard, vaguely, while distracted and fetching a beer.

We need to face the fact that who runs the country is less important than being satisfied with the new season of programs on TV. If the U.S. President was smart, he would get Congress to pass a bill giving him final say on what programs are on TV. Caesar realized that he could stay in power by controlling the entertainment in the Coliseum. He was able to change the Roman Empire from a republic to a dictatorship by giving the masses good entertainment; why can't we do the same? Wouldn't it be worthwhile to give up the right to vote if we could have better programs? Voting has been on a decline since the invention of the TV, so why not just stop it all together? Voting is, in theory, the voice of the majority instructing our elected officials on issues they believe important. But, when the majority doesn't vote, are we not going against our theory of government by giving the minority rule over our future? Voting has become a practice of a minority of the population given the right to vote based on the linear concept of age. It is not actually performing the intended function anyway, so we could certainly do away with it.

Getting back to the TV's role in our lives, I have been scrutinizing those commercials and taking an unofficial census of their content. I have noticed some very interesting trends in commercials. The commercial is designed to cater to those people most able to purchase or interested in purchasing the products that are touted in them. Carefully compiled statistics and demographics on these facts let the advertisers know where to spend their dollar. Since the advertisers try to make the most out of each dollar spent, you must assume that they are reaching out for those people with the liquid capital available to purchase the products they are hawking.

My census of commercials and their content would indicate that women have most of the purchasing power in our country. The most prevalent commercials are for products used by woman. These products are, for the most part, hygiene products of one form or another. These products are for treatment of either the epidermis or one of the orifices with which women are equipped. Many of the products are for a cure of one or more of the maladies besetting women's genitalia. These products are either to fix a problem such as a yeast infection or to eliminate an odor caused by or coupled with the fact that they have a vagina.

One of the major breakthroughs in recent history seems to be the discovery of Lotrimin, an antifungal medication that cures yeast infections. The breakthrough is not the actual discovery of Lotrimin, but the discovery of pharmaceutical companies that, if they pay off the right government officials, can get this miracle cure out to people as an over-the-counter medication, eliminating doctors as middlemen and dramatically increasing profits. I have watched, with amazement, the progress in the area of yeast infections, or should I say the progress of the efficacy of this medication in treating yeast infections.

At the onset of the commercials for these products, it was claimed that they could cure a yeast infection in seven days. This was portrayed as a marvelous accomplishment, and everyone except the manufacturers were in awe of the expedience of the cure. I judged this to be a great accomplishment by the obvious excitement of the actress bringing us the wonderful news. As in any great capitalist societies where there is an opportunity to make money, competition is inevitable. Soon another company was advertising that they also had a seven-day cure for the dreaded yeast infection, but theirs was easier

GETTING OLD

to apply, which gave them the marketing edge. Soon the first company retaliated with an even easier application method. This battle of methodology went on for some time with each touting a better way. Once all possible application methods had been exhausted, just when the standard-bearer for application method seemed to be winning the competition, some genius in the marketing department of the apparent loser hit upon another avenue of sales promotion: the time it takes to affect an eradication of this incapacitating affliction.

Time then became the focus of the competition. The time it took to cure the disease dominated everyone's ad campaign. It began to sound a lot like *Name That Tune*.

"I can cure that yeast infection in four days!"

"I can cure that yeast infection in three days!"

"I can cure that yeast infection in one dose!"

Assumedly, the only thing faster than one dose would be no doses, which is an impossibility, so thàt seems to be the end-all, be-all of yeast infection cures. Now that they have gotten the yeast infection cure down to almost a non-problem, perhaps we can move on to the lesser problems of life. I am convinced that if every disease known to mankind could somehow be restricted to the vaginal region, we could eliminate all diseases in about three years.

The yeast infection cure rate is good news, but since it hasn't been eliminated altogether, there is still that bit of awkward time from application to cure, a major concern to those people so intently concerned with the vagina. That time when a detectable odor may be emitted and found objectionable to those around you. This is another great concern according to those advertisers who bring such wonderful matters to our attention. The product to use during this time is designed "not just to mask odor but to eliminate it." This product is a modern marvel of some advertising genius. It is the universal eliminator of odors everywhere from the toilet to the tennis shoe to the refrigerator to the drain. It can kill any odor anywhere. It is BAKING SODA.

This modern miracle has replaced the desirable 'Lemon Scent' of the Seventies and Eighties as the most sought after odor remedy known to humankind. You can spritz it, sprinkle it, pour it, blow it into any crack, crevice, or cranny that is emitting any odor that is offensive and immediately eliminate the odor. You can open a box of it and set it in your refrigerator: no more odor. It is truly a wonderful product. The advertisers of this product have taken it from an item you may have purchased one box of in ten years to something you cannot live without in your daily lives. I can still remember the box my mother had in the cupboard all of those years. No one but she knew what it was for, and it just got older and crustier looking year by year. Too bad that we had no idea of its potency; we could have put it in my brother's tennis shoes.

Well, to get back to the female condition, I am glad that females have this open forum of television to get news on every vaginal affliction that may occur. I am also glad that it, being TV, is a visual medium, and that the radio is not the vehicle of choice to bring such news to the listener. If you were just to close your eyes when these commercials are presented, you would see what I mean. The slogans and descriptions offer some interesting mental images, and I wonder what images blind people who don't use these products conjure up. With my eyes closed, I can see "the maximum in comfort and protection" as a woman sitting in a large overstuffed armchair and holding an automatic rifle, with an alert Doberman on either side of her. I can see a panty liner with wings as something of a cargo ship with hydrofoils, whisking Victoria's Secrets from some obscure eastern dictatorship to the waiting mobs of female shoppers.

Darwin's theory of evolution says that all species develop over time to eliminate threats to their ultimate survival. If this is true, given the circumstances portrayed on TV concerning the objectionable nature of the female reproductive organs, I can visualize the repositioning of the vagina over years of evolution to a position as far from the olfactory organs as possible. This could entail the lengthening of the torso and a shortening of the legs in order to affect this revision in the female form. I can picture that someday, if all conditions remain the same, human females could take on the appearance of penguins.

Although the vagina is of major concern to big business and to woman alike as the first orifice of concern, it is by far not the last. For as long as humankind has realized that chemicals of one kind or another are effective in curing ailments and killing hostile organisms that invade us and use us as hosts, humans have been experimenting with which orifice to stick the chemicals in to get the most immediate and beneficial results. The realization that these orifices are important avenues to the inner organs has also spurred the desire to keep these orifices in good working order. Not only do we have the medications to treat the inner maladies of humans but also remedies for the more superficial parts of the physical being. As these outer reaches have not been considered as important as the inner body. many of the remedies for the maladies of the orifices and epidermis have been left to what is called the over- the-counter pharmaceutical market. Such things as runny noses, watery eyes, earaches, tooth pain, itchy scalps, itchy crotches, itchy feet, and the pain and itch of hemorrhoids have all been relegated to a process of healing that eliminates doctors. We have established a direct relationship between the manufacturer and the consumer. Televion carries this relationship forward. The manufacturer graphically describes your malady, graphically explains what their product can do for you, and then tells you where to get the product. For many years, this format served people of both sexes, equally. The information-gathering of the computer has recently enhanced the ability of these companies. I believe it has now been determined that woman buy most of the available products and do most of the shopping, so most of the products are advertised to appeal to female purchasers. The new strategy is to not only appeal to women as the purchasers but to state that these products are designed specifically *for women*, even if they are universally effective on man and beast. We now have products for female scalps, female athlete's foot, female hemorrhoids, and female sweating, all being advertised as effective only on woman.

As is made evident by these commercials, the female purchasing power is endless and care of the female is of major concern, yet in all of the studies on earning power, women are said to make less money than men do. Could it be that women are involved in some secret under-the-counter drug selling? Could it be that these woman are involved in a secret plot to buy "for women only" remedies and then resell them in a black market to men who sweat, have scalp itch, and athlete's foot?

Even commercials for products not necessarily consumed by women are designed to cater to women as the purchasers. These commercials are for products consumed by children and/or pets but are definitely designed to attract the female as the purchaser. The next most popular group to sway is the children, just in case Mom didn't get the message. Finally, the last group catered to is the male. The commercials designed for the male viewing audience usuallly address what to buy for a female.

To only go this far would not be a complete breakdown of the demographic and statistical views of groups to which the commercials are aimed, and further analysis is necessary to get a true picture. There are certain maladies and conditions, both physical and social, which would further separate these rather large groups into subgroups more easily targeted.

I have also seen a disturbing trend in advertising with origins in the television situation comedy that has since evolved from harmless fun to serious propaganda. Sometime after the women's rights movement began, a certain fear invaded the male psyche. The ever-growing power of the women's movement toward equality and all of the accompanying propaganda struck a deep fear in males that the guiles once used to elicit sex would no longer be effective. The power-based system once enjoyed by the male was rapidly diminishing and only in those few male strongholds – topless bars and golf courses – could a man still be a man.

Women also gradually began to take over the previously male-dominated field of television advertising. The once authoritarian father image that used to inform and tout almost every product began disappearing from television commercials about the same time that the *Father Knows Best* image began imploding. The implosion soon took men from the all-knowing patriarch and wisdom purveyor to a blithering idiot who relies exclusively on females for sustenance.

The reason for this shift in male image is the same reason for all of the actions of men where women are concerned: the fear that if they do not comply with female wishes, sex will be a thing of the past. The writers that portray men as the idiot, such as "Tim the Tool Man," suffer from the same reasoning as the men that tote jewelry home for birthdays, Christmas, Mother's Day and Halloween: the nagging fear that sex will be withheld.

This segment of the male population, men who want to buy things for women, is catered to on a regular basis. It seems to be the middle class American male's plight, to be considered an idiot who can be parted from his money by dangling the one thing in front of him he cannot resist.

This chapter is about aging, so let's get back to it. As I said before getting a bit distracted, as we physically age, a progression of medications, remedies, and elixirs are first peddled to maintain youth, and then when that is no longer possible because of the aging process, they are hawked to magically make us look or feel younger. The clock ticks, and soon we are looking for products to prop up an aging body and soothe an ailing spirit. All of these are cash sales for the very patient pharmaceutical companies and doctors alike.

I, along with you, am aging rapidly considering the miniscule amount of time we have compared to the life of the universe. We are a flash on the clock of time. We are only allotted that millisecond, and we want it to last as long as possible. This is what makes all of the prescription drug peddling a very profitable business. The explosion of humanity, called "Boomers," is pushing medical marvels and the search for new products to a new, never-ending high.

One product that has great promise for a future once it has gained acceptance is "Depends." The makers and advertisers of this product have not yet dared to explore its potential. Perhaps they soon will. I

◄ THE BIG BOOK OF DAN

believe that once accepted, this product will reach consumer groups never before considered. The possibilities are endless. Although designed to cope with incontinence there are so many other situations that would be fitting for just such a device.

Let's say you are going to your local sports bar to watch the game. Game day guarantees a big crowd. You arrive early to get a prime seat, one that you don't want to give up. Naturally, you begin drinking beer as soon as you arrive. As the place fills up, so do you. As game time arrives, so does a certain urge. You can't leave a full bottle at your seat to denote your presence; someone might drink it or put a cigarette butt out in it. You can't leave an empty chair the seat mongers will choose to think you deserted. How then do you relieve yourself without losing your place? Now, if you had at your disposal a product that would solve this horrific problem, would you not use it? Well here it is! The wonderful, ultra absorbent, designed to fit snug in the legs, maximum in comfort and protection "Game- Day Depends." Resplendent in team colors and logo and bearing the number of your favorite player, it can solve all of your game-day worries. No more having to miss plays and waiting for half time to relieve yourself, no more rushing in and out during commercials, no more bouncing on your seat or jiggling your knee trying to postpone the inevitable. Now you can watch every stimulating moment, drink to your heart's content, and never leave your seat.

This single example of a cutting-edge consumer) application shows just one aspect of the usefulness of this particular product. There are so many other possibilities: for snow skiers, no more tramping through the lodge in those stiff awkward boots or getting through all those layers of clothes; for joggers, no more looking for a bush when over exertion brings on that instant need; for swimmers (well actually for other swimmers around you), for the couch-potato's elimination of that last act of exertion.

We grow older physically but still have a youthful mentality. We are suspended in a Never-Never Land: never-never grow old. We all cling to our youth, some more tenaciously than others. There are

GETTING OLD

always those people who think that by dressing drastically younger than their years, they will be viewed as being the age their costume indicates. Toupeed or balding-with-a pony-tail men strut around in leather motorcycle clothes, women who have long since lost the first blush dress in clothes that would only look sexy on a girl one-third their age and in much better shape than the years have left them. Speculation leads me to believe that at some point in time, if these examples cling that tenaciously to youth, there might possibly be a market for a Thong Depends. All of these possibilities await those with an open mind and an ample supply of zinc oxide ointment. Soon there may even be a Depends driver's model for those who want to get to that vacation destination even faster.

For many of us Baby Boomers who passed through the natural elixirs of the early seventies, life has gone full circle. During the seventies, many found that the natural herbs available at that time had a tranquilizing effect. A true grass-roots movement was born in which the roots were about the only thing not ingested. From those days of all-natural, we progressed to the all-manmade-medication, and now we are heading back to "all natural" with a vengeance. One of the many products that has become popular is ginseng, which advertisers claim gives you extra energy, something we all need considering credit card debt and middle age libidinous activities. Another popular product is St. John's Wort, which is said to be nature's answer to Valium. It's great that we now have all-natural uppers and downers, and they're legal, too.

In investigating some of the comtemporary natural cures, I came upon one that has somehow escaped the popularity of those mentioned above. It is a remedy perfected by a little known and somewhat obscure group of people who settled in Louisiana some time ago. I thought an in-depth explanation and history would be in order.

A long time ago, the Cajuns migrated from Nova Scotia to Louisiana seeking religious freedom. They were not the only group to migrate to Louisiana seeking freedom. There was a small group of Jewish people led by a courageous fellow named Rabbi Adam Winkleman who also

THE BIG BOOK OF DAN

migrated to Louisiana searching for their freedom. Not the religious freedom sought by the Cajuns, but pharmaceutical freedom. They believed in natural remedies, remedies that society shunned and that were spurned by a medical community that held sway over the legal system. And this was a legal system that prosecuted anyone who did not practice medicine exactly as the medical community believed it should be practiced.

This small group believed so strongly in natural remedies that they moved from the more populated area of Nova Scotia to the northern reaches of Nova Scotia where they could practice without prosecution. This proved to be impractical because the ingredients necessary were scarce to impossible to obtain in this foreboding land.

Rabbi Winkleman realized quickly that this was an untenable situation and began searching for a new place for his enclave to settle that would provide the plant stuff needed for their natural remedy practices. He heard that the Cajuns found their niche in a world where popularity outweighed good sense, an isolated place called Louisiana. He decided to relocate his people to this land where they would be free to practice and experiment with natural healing.

They began the journey by loading small boats with their belongings and heading down the Nova River to Southern Nova Scotia. They reached Southern Nova Scotia after going through a series of locks. The famous Nova Locks were their last obstacles, but once through the locks they were in the southern end of the country and preparing to head even further south.

Rabbi Winkleman negotiated a great deal: a package for the ocean journey to New York and the complete land package to Louisiana. They landed in Baton Rouge after six months of arduous travel. They quickly left the city to find their little piece of freedom out in the secluded bayous, far from the scrutiny of the medical community.

Up a small river and far from any other settlement, Rabbi Winkleman found the place that he felt fitted their needs. He located a lush, green bit of land with abundant plants used for natural remedies. It was a marvelous place, first seen by an explorer of the

18th century named Wunder Howe and named for him. It was called Howe's Bayou (Pronounced How's By You). This was immediately recognized as the perfect place to practice natural healing.

The natural flora of Howe's Bayou abundantly provided the standard remedies, such as St. John's Wort, that were widely used not only by Rabbi Winkleman's community but by all of the poor people throughout the bayous. Also available were wondrous cures perfected by the black population during their many years of enslavement and poverty. A growing awareness of all of these medicinal ingredients, new to the Rabbi, led to greater curiosity on his part to investigate and experiment with other possible cures. He experimented furiously with all types of plants, barks, tubers and minerals to find their effects on human miseries.

One of Rabbi Winkleman's greatest successes was the discovery of an epidermally-applied, multi-purpose cure. This cure, although peculiar, proved to be effective for many physical and mental conditions. The application method that promoted maximum efficacy was also rather peculiar.

This most famous cure that the Rabbi discovered was contained in a moss that grows on the tops of old rotting cypress trunks in the bayou. The efficacy of the product depended on the removal procedure. The entire growth of moss had to be removed in one piece from the top of the trunk. This required a rather careful procedure that the Rabbi was familiar with, but on a smaller scale.

The moss needs to be kept moist prior to use in order for proper application. This application is rather tricky, and to maximize the effect, it needs to be used over an extended period. Even with all of the handling, packaging and application problems, this medication was highly sought after and used by many people.

The moss was prescribed to calm aggressive behavior and settle nervous conditions caused by living in social groups. This wonder drug was most effective on mental conditions ranging from mild depression to raving paranoia. The unexpected actions of removing blemishes and wrinkles and growing hair, leaving the user looking

THE BIG BOOK OF DAN

years younger, were wonderful side effects of the extended use of this medication. The added benefits explained its resulting overuse.

This topical cure, still available today, is applied by taking the entire moss plant and placing it on top of the head, rolling it out like a stocking cap over the face and head, down to the neck. The moss, in its processed condition, is translucent and air permeable so the patient can see through it and breathe through it, making it possible to wear for long periods. The moss clings to the skin and shrinks slightly. For these reasons, it is necessary to have the moss removed by a general practitioner. It has to be cut away carefully and peeled from the face. The only known adverse side effect of this miracle cure was a brown ring around the neck where it stopped, exposing the skin to oxygen, but regular users were willing to risk this to get the healing effect of the moss

This cure bears the name of its founder in tribute to his years of research. If you are interested in using this miracle cure for any of its medicinal benefits, it can be found in any herbal remedy shop under its generic name, Rabbi Winkleman's Foreskin.

There are now so many products available to postpone, turn back, and deny the aging process, it must be a common belief that growing old is a bad thing. We are caught in the search for youth but have perfected products that help us live longer. More and more people are living to ages well past the norm of twenty years ago. In actuality we are not postponing old age; we are ensuring that more people get there. To complicate matters, we spend our youths overindulging in every bad habit that will shorten our lives, and by the time we get to middle age, we are in a sickly state, relying on the elixirs available to postpone the inevitable – death. It may be true that more people are living longer, but it must also be true that by the time they finally succumb to some illness they are sicker than most dying people were twenty years ago.

The younger a person is, the younger old is, and the older you get, the older old becomes. The younger a person is, the less precious each day is, and the older one becomes, the more precious is each day.

GETTING OLD

The physical aging process does not appear to be connected to the mental aging process. We all are the centers of our own universe and always have been. What is apparently old to onlookers is not old to our mentality. The calendar used to mark the days and years is only pertinent to a society that depends on time for its functioning. Age is relative to spirit and has nothing to do with a calendar or a timeline. It has everything to do with the person inside us.

The great thing about coming from a time period when the culmination of events led to a procreative explosion is that I will have so much company while growing old. With the advent of so many medical miracles postponing the final outcome of life, more people will live longer and longer. The longer people live, the wider the range of that wonderful time between young and old, called middle age.

Middle aged is a term seldom used now because people want to be considered young until they are old. Yet it is a marvelous period of life, a place that everyone who is not young or old should visit and enjoy. It is the time when the folly of youth is over but the onset of old age is not yet upon us. It is the balance point between the yin of youth and the yang of old age, and the time when the kids are finally independent and the house is paid for, the career has peaked, and striving to meet expectations has ended. Happily, at this time the body is not yet ready for the sedentary life of old age, and life is most comfortable. I think it is the best time I have ever had, and I am less willing to leave this middle age part of life than any period in time I have lived through. The only reason to leave this period in my life is the calendar and a concept of time meaningless in the greater scheme of the universe.

Old is inevitable and actually desirable when you consider the alternative to growing old. There is only one way out, and I would rather it be later than sooner. Despite all of the miracle drugs and potions we concoct, it is our fate to end like every other animal on the planet. The only difference is, when they go, they contribute their bodies back to the earth, providing food and fertilizer for new beginnings, and life goes on. We are boxed up in the hopes that we can still participate, if only on holidays.

A View from the Bottom

I had my teeth all cleaned you see,
in prepping for a colonoscopy.
I'd hate for that report to come back,
saying all they found was plaque.

Growing in Age

(Intentionally large typeface)

When I became bifocular,
I also became more jocular.
It seems when sight starts to blur,
vision becomes more pure.

When I want to make the scene,
I take my glucosamine.
It's a time when low blood pressure
becomes something to treasure.

When someone yells, "Hey your fly is down,"
I smile and zip up without turning around.
I have an insight, a mystical vision,
four times a night in the bathroom, whizzin'.

Passing gas may bring a surprise,
being cautious in public is always wise.
With hearing failing a little each day,
what I hear is not always what you say.

In plaid pants, striped shirts and argyle socks,
We'll strut in the park like proud old peacocks.
No, not me, you'll whimper and cry,
but you'll be there with us when time zooms by.

(Oh, I forgot–your memory–forget about it.)

I Want to Go Low and Slow

You might surmise,
upon my demise,
I will have a final request.
Please no cold crypt or plot,
no cremation hot,
the thought leaves me distressed.

I would like to be lovingly dressed,
and gently, with pure oils, caressed.
Please rub me with spices that bite,
then put me on low and slow,
at about 200 or so,
and tend to me all through the night.

For my final wish,
bring a covered dish,
and eat your fill with glee.
A thoughtful device,
to celebrate twice,
the jubilant passing of me.

Tom — My Remembrance

IT HAS BEEN a long time since I have seen him, a longer time since I slept with Tom, and yet I remember him in the most distinct detail. He was my hero, my friend, at times my adversary, but always my brother.

When I say slept with him, I must say it was commonplace to sleep in the same room as your brother. Not only did we sleep in the same room but in the same bed. Dave, my other brother, slept in the single bed across the room. Across the room was not that far. We could reach out and smack each other at any time, and we often did. Most evenings a barrage of pillows, spitballs, peas, and rubber bands flew in all directions. When all of the missiles were launched and lost in the bedding, a few volleys of insults and laughter usually followed until the noise level rose high enough to bring admonishment from Ma or threats my from father.

We began sleeping three to a room when my sister Rose Mary was born; I was nine, Tom eleven, and Dave fourteen. Before Rose Mary came along, Tom and I slept in the same room. Our bedroom consisted of a small, square, hardwood floor big enough for a double bed, a single bed, a bureau, a chair, and a pile of dirty clothes that got larger at night and smaller during the day as Ma tried to keep up with the never-ending laundry. We had the luxury of two windows, one near each bed, letting in the cool air on summer nights. Air conditioning was unheard of in our neighborhood but not missed. Those two windows provided many memories that may have been missed if manufactured cool air were available. Our window was at the foot of our bed. In winter, a stiff breeze whistled through this window. We stayed huddled under cover, as far from it as we could. In the summer, though, the window was a welcomed convenience providing refreshing cool air to sweltering kids as evening drifted into night, and we fell into sleep.

THE BIG BOOK OF DAN

A period existed between the spring warming and the end of school when days grew longer. Unfortunately, our bedtime still came under the school days rule. Eight o'clock found us lying in bed long before nightfall. With the windows open wide, we would listen to our friends yelling, "Ollie ollie ox in free" or asking "Red rover, red rover can Billie come over?" Raucous laughter and cajoling drifted up from the street. Our friends' parents were less stringent about the laws of child rearing. As we were a handful, I am sure the bedtime law had something to do with tucking us into our cell after an exercise period in order to maintain parental sanity.

Although school weeknights meant an early curfew, weekends were a little less stringent. Our parents allowed us to stay up to watch *Ozzie and Harriet, Father Knows Best, Walt Disney Presents,* and other family programs. We popped popcorn and spread blankets on the floor, huddling together to watch these fictitious portrayals of family life. We lay in bed wishing that what we had would somehow resemble those programs. The harsh truth was that our family life resembled *The Honeymooners,* but with considerably more physical violence. We were baby boomers, a condition arrived at by the mating of two people who shared the most traumatic situations that you could imagine. People who lived for some years apart, our parents were thrust back together with no counseling and expected to carry on as normal, social humans. Tom was fortunate. He developed the skill of the joke and could make uncomfortable situations into humorous ones.

One Sunday on *Walt Disney*, we saw a demonstration of a chain reaction. A guy sat in the middle of hundreds of loaded mousetraps, each one with a ping-pong ball sitting on the trip mechanism. He threw one ping-pong ball in the air. As the ball struck a trap, it tripped the trap and launched that ball until hundreds of balls were tripping more and more traps. It reached a marvelous crescendo and then slowed until the last trap tripped. The vision of all of those balls tripping traps, and trap-tripping launching more balls, stuck. We both knew that, if ever given an opportunity, we would try to duplicate the feat.

As I mentioned earlier, the window at the foot of our bed brought cooling breezes, a welcome relief as the summer nights heated up. We positioned ourselves with our heads in the window to take advantage of the wisps of air blowing in. With no fans to move the air, the room became stifling at times. Through our window, we not only had pleasant, cool air blowing over us, but we had a porthole into the workings of our little slice of neighborhood.

Every house had a front porch and a well-used, outdoor living space. When houses were as intolerably hot at night inside as the outside was during the day, our neighbors sought relief outdoors. We were privy to many events that perhaps unwitting adults did not suspect. For one thing, we learned that we were not the only dysfunctional group of souls on the block. We often heard little stabbing jabs and ill-tempered remarks rising up from the porches below. On occasion, a knockdown, drag-out brawl would bring the cops racing down the street to calm tempers and restore order. Intertwined with the bickering and brawling was a bit of amorous foreplay and slap and tickle.

We found out that we were not the only eavesdroppers and interlopers in the neighborhood. Dale, four doors away, was lucky enough to be across the street from two sisters from Holland who watched TV in the altogether. Each of our friends that had bedrooms facing the other side of the street had different views and different stories. All those nights spent side by side sharing adventures bonded us closely enough to last us through all the rivalries of our daytime lives.

Tom, the daredevil of the family, spent the summer of 1953 convalescing from injuries after being hit by a car. Only five, I remember it clearly, because that year a tornado touched down on our street. We huddled in the basement while Tom, packed in sandbags at the hospital, watched the neighborhood swirl by his window. The debris, cleared by the time the hospital released him, left our once tree-lined streets barren of foliage over five feet tall. How fortunate we were to have a clear, open area to play baseball and football, not having to dodge three-foot diameter trunks or worry about overhanging limbs that might deflect that home run ball.

When eight years old, Tom sold the winning ticket for the church raffle. A Lyman sixteen-foot runabout won by our uncle gave Tom an open invitation to go fishing with Uncle Blackie, along with a brand new bicycle for selling the winning ticket. The bike was destroyed a week after he received it. Dared to ride the bike down a steep hill, Tom lost control, went off the paved road into a field, hit a stump, flipped the bike, and broke three ribs. He came home dragging the bike behind him. He stumbled through the back door, flopped on the floor, and whimpered, "I can't breathe, I can't breathe." After a trip to the local emergency room, he returned home to heal. Of course, this gave Dave and me endless opportunities to razz him. For months, every time he came into the room we would fall on the floor and whimper, "I can't breathe, I can't breathe." Eventually the razzing wore thin, and we gave it up.

One particularly harsh winter, our family benefactor, Uncle Clarence, provided Tom and I an opportunity to fulfill our *Walt Disney* dream. Every Christmas, Uncle Clarence gave each of us $20 in a Merry Christmas money envelope. Receiving $20 under any circumstances gave us a momentary high; $20 was hard to come by. We knew Ma targeted it for winter coats, gloves and other necessities. This particular year Ma didn't collect the cash; we didn't know why, and we didn't ask for fear she would come to her senses, and it would be gone. We skulked around for a couple of days waiting for the hammer to fall, but it never did. We believed, or maybe just hoped, this presented a clear sign that the cash was ours to spend.

We did not leave the house with a target purchase in mind. Sloshing through the snow, we talked about all kinds of possibilities. Sears and Roebuck lay two miles from home. We had plenty of time to explore the potential of two flush, young guys out for the day. We spent hours picking up toys, playing with them, putting them back, watching TV in the appliance department, and chasing through the

TOM – MY REMEMBRANCE

candy department. We finally burst through the double doors and out to the cold slushy sidewalk with store security hot on our tails. Back on the street with $40 and our day ending, we felt the need to make a large capital expenditure before Mom realized her error and we lost our cash.

Directly across from Sears, the big red Western Auto sign beckoned to us. We walked down to the crosswalk, sloshed through the puddles and slush, and walked back to the Western Auto. A whirlwind of shopping lust ensued. When it was over, we owned a 50-calibre machine gun, two Frisbees, and $32 in mousetraps and ping-pong balls. Elated with our purchases, we talked all the way home about our big plan to duplicate the *Walt Disney* chain-reaction demonstration. We burst through the door anxious to set up the demonstration, only to be intercepted by Ma and forced to reveal our purchases. The $32 purchase of mousetraps and ping-pong balls turned into shoes, boots, gloves, socks, and underwear the next day.

In her reminiscences, Ma included only one other story as often as the mousetrap story. Our father, who we secretly referred to as 'the old man,' had decided to teach us a lesson about managing money, or maybe it was just a contrivance to torture us. He bought a case of Little Tom soda pop, put it in the refrigerator in the basement, and placed a bank-like can with a slot in the top on the refrigerator. Each bottle cost a dime, and when the supply had been depleted, he would buy another case. The pop disappeared at a rapid rate, much to David's and my surprise. We knew *we* could not afford to buy all this soda, but in three days, all of the pop was gone. We shook the can a few times: no clatter, no jingle. Dave and I waited with great anticipation for the can to be opened. The old man removed the lid, turned it over, and shook out 24 neatly-folded pieces of paper, each saying, *I.O.U. 10 cents,* and signed by Tom. It was the first and last case of Little Tom soda pop appearing in our basement refrigerator, but the laugh it produced lasted a long time.

As Tom and I grew, he became muscular and very athletic. He was good at everything – baseball, football, wrestling, running, and

THE BIG BOOK OF DAN

boxing. I did not fare well in competition with him and for the most part did not even try.

Once a year, in the spring after a long winter of tension brewed by teasing, picking, and aggravating, he and I would have a fistfight. This was always a sudden event. A storm of emotion erupted instantaneously somewhere in the neighborhood. We would fight and walk, fight and walk for blocks, constantly moving so that a well-meaning neighbor could not break it up. We fought until we reached home, usually accompanied by a troupe of friends acting as cheerleaders and preventing any interference. When we arrived home, we would get ice from the refrigerator, wrap it in dishtowels, and nurse our bruises. We knew the fighting was over until next spring.

Our relationship orbits were elliptical for a while as we each discovered new horizons. Tom graduated from high school and started an apprenticeship with the Ironworkers Union. He worked the high steel of bridge and building construction for two years. He decided it was too dangerous when the fifth member of the crew he worked with lost his life falling five stories on the Federal Building in downtown Cleveland. Tom moved on to a new adventure.

Tom decided it would be a safer career move to become a Marine than to remain an Ironworker. He went off to boot camp and transformed himself into Tom the Marine. Lance Corporal Thomas W. Dulik came home with orders to report for duty in two weeks, shipping out to Viet Nam. Home from the Navy for two weeks, he slept during the day and bar hopped at night with Dave. I acted as chauffeur and finance man when they were too drunk to drive, and too broke to pay. I also provided most of the civilian clothes, aftershave, and toiletries necessary to make them presentable to the girls.

I drove Tom to Washington, D.C., to catch a Greyhound back to camp after his two-week sabbatical. We spent most of the eight hours driving in silence, only grunting as necessary to signal piss calls and food breaks. I was angry about the two weeks of interruptions in my love life, unreimbursed gas expenses, and wardrobe damages from cigarette burns and puke stains. He was probably worried about sur-

TOM – MY REMEMBRANCE

viving his impetuous decision to join. Upon arrival, he bolted from the car. Running to the station, duffle bag slung over his shoulder, he waved his hand above his head to say goodbye.

Tom had been "in country," a term for being in Viet Nam, for three weeks – just long enough to receive a letter from him and to ship requested supplies back. My girlfriend and I went on a Memorial Day picnic with friends. We spent the day drinking beer, grilling burgers, and playing ball. It was like any other Memorial Day picnic, nothing out of the ordinary. I dropped her off at her house and went home a little drunk and a lot satisfied. Walking through the door, crying parents confronted me. I knew what was coming. A freckle-faced, red-haired Marine Corps Corporal in bright and crisp full-dress uniform began to speak. Somewhere between "I regret to tell you" and "Viet Nam" a blister formed on my soul. By the time Taps sounded and the third volley of seven was fired, that blister had turned into a thick, hard callous. Tom, a part of my existence for so many years, was gone.

Drafted in February of 1969, I became an unwilling yet resigned participant in the Army of the United States of America. When I received my draft notice, my father, a veteran of WWII, offered to drive me to Canada. I decided to take my chances and see how fate would play out. Basic training took place in Fort Campbell, Kentucky. Nearing completion, names were called to report for M-16 training. This guaranteed a ticket to a long plane ride and an unpleasant time in a far-off land. At the end of basic, assignment to Fort Polk, Louisiana, placed a sure bet that the next step was the war zone.

Fort Polk shared the same parallel as Viet Nam and had remarkably similar weather. Sweat rings from armpits to belt line appeared on your shirt before noon. The nights were sultry, with night creatures flying and crawling everywhere. Days, punctuated with sudden thunderstorms, often ended in clouds of steam. A training company for vehicle drivers became my assignment due to some trickery during in-processing. Our bus arrived late in the day. We all had orders to report to an infantry training company for Advanced Individual

Training. It was obvious to us that we were destined to become cannon fodder in a short time. My friends and I got at the end of the line for in-processing. With the arrival of every busload of trainees, we moved to the end of an ever-growing line. At 2:00 a.m., we finally reached the processing point, and with no more room in the infantry barracks, a valid driver's license provided a passport to M.O.S. 86A10: truck-driving school. Without that license, I would have become a cook.

Reserved for on-the-job training, the last two weeks of basic training were spent driving for a regular Army company. We already had our orders; I would be leaving for Viet Nam on July 17. Resigned to my fate, I did not look forward to breaking the news to my family and brand new wife. I postponed it for the first week, trying to formulate the least upsetting way to let them know.

After bouncing around in a jeep or deuce and a half (a big ass Army truck) ten hours a day, I began to feel a soreness just above my butt crack. I went on sick call when it was still a sore spot, and an unsympathetic sergeant, screening for malingerers, pressed on it. He didn't think it anything significant and sent me back to work. The area changed from moderate soreness to a sore lump that enlarged as the hours passed. After the third day, no position gave me comfort, and sleep was impossible. I reported to my training company and again went on sick call. The doctor prodded the now golf-ball-sized lump, and, after some loud whimpering and under-my-breath swearing, took pity on me, and sent me to the hospital.

Fort Polk had been built for a segregated army, with all of the amenities such as the hospital, the main PX, and the main movie theater on the white side of the fort; unfortunately, I was on the black side. I endured a seven-mile ride from one side of the base to the other on a stiff, sparsely padded bus seat. Nobody stood on an Army bus.

At the bus stop, I encountered a new inductee from the boot camp company down the road. He seemed happier than any new soldier should be. I inquired as to the origins of his happiness, and he explained to me that he had a lump just above his butt crack that had raised during training. He had been to the hospital last week where they lanced it and healed the infection temporarily. He now needed surgery to remove the pilonidal cyst causing the infection. He also conveyed to me a discussion he had with the doctor. If he refused the operation, they would have no choice but to let him out of the Army. As we finished our conversation, the bus pulled up to take me to the hospital and my eventual discharge from the Army. As the bus pulled away, I looked back and saw the smiling face of my angel, Tom, and his energetic wave.

Goodbye.

Over the years, he has presented himself to me in various disguises and helped me out of some tough spots when I needed it most. He had different faces under different circumstances but always the same presence that I knew from so long ago.

To address the callus on my soul, I am 61 years old, and it has worn down over the years. It is much thinner now, whittled smaller by loving relationships, kind acts, and an understanding that comes with age. I miss my brother every day and will until I see him again. I feel the uselessness of war after so many skirmishes fought with the promise of peace. I feel sorry for all the families who have lost loved ones. I am sick at heart hearing the news and names of soldiers killed, and knowing that people have become casually accustomed to those announcements. The solid memory of my brother stands by me throughout.

This Nose of Killer Man Jaro

Punched with a right it bent right,
this nose of Killer Man Jaro.
Hooked from the left it bent left,
this nose of Killer Man Jaro.
It's pulped, pitted, bright red,
this nose of Killer Man Jaro.
The standout feature of his head,
this nose of Killer Man Jaro.
A flattened nose, a wide-spread nose,
this nose of Killer Man Jaro.
A fighter's nose, a famous nose,
this nose of Killer Man Jaro.
It's taken one too many blows,
this nose of Killer Man Jaro.
Now it's in its final repose,
this nose of Killer Man Jaro.

What Are Words Worth, Longfellow?

"What are words worth, Longfellow?
Before I lay down my MasterCard,
do I buy them by the piece or the yard?
Please, what are words worth, Longfellow?"

"Well, let me tell you, William.
In that bin is what we call the letter.
Buy an assortment and string them together
That's the cheapest we have, William."

"Again, what are words worth, Longfellow?
I want to get something good
to use around the neighborhood.
Please tell me, what are words worth, Longfellow?"

"If that's what you really want, Will.
Those boxes have words all alphabetized,
some not so good, some highly prized.
That's one step up, Will."

"I looked through those, Longfellow.
I need some strung together,
some that sound really clever.
What are those words worth, Longfellow?"

"Look here now, Will.
Over on the rack are what we call cards,
with sentimental sayings from unknown bards.
Price is marked on the back, Will."

"No, no those won't do, Longfellow.
I need something with lots of pages,
you know, something pithy that engages.
What are those words worth, Longfellow?"

"Okay, now I know what you want, Bill.
What you want is called a book.
Look on the shelves in that nook.
Those are getting up in price, Bill."

"Please tell me, what are those words worth, Longfellow?
There are so many to choose from,
please help me, I feel dumb.
I'll pay extra, what are those words worth, Longfellow?"

"Billy, when you came in, I wasn't sure,
but what you want we loosely call literature.
Now that I know, let me be your guide,
fold back the covers to see what's inside."

"On the top shelf are mystery, mayhem, and gore,
I can throw in sex for a little more.
Modern romance is in demand,
I, myself, find them a little bland.
Political commentary by self-serving buttholes,
but boy, they end up with gigantic bankrolls.

Self- improvement, bought by the distraught,
just a few customers, but they buy a lot.
On the bottom shelf, land of dust bunnies and gnomes,
those two thin books are what we call poems."

"So tell me, what are poems worth, Longfellow?"

"Billy, mayhem, mystery, and gore
can all be had for $15.94.
Throw in the sex, it's always fun –
that will be $17.91.
Modern Romance, gals think it's heaven,
I'll sell you that for $12.87.
Political commentary, by some strange bedmate,
will grab all your cash at $11.98.
Self-improvement from the latest guru,
you could buy that for, I think, $10.62.
Now poetry, I'd sound a bit cliché,
if I said to you it was priceless, eh?
If that's all I sold, I couldn't survive;
I'll give you both books for $1.95"

"I expect to pass through this world but once. Any good therefore that I can do, or any kindness or abilities that I can show to any fellow creature, let me do it now. Let me not defer it or neglect it, for I shall not pass this way again."

William Penn

CPSIA information can be obtained
at www.ICGtesting.com
Printed in the USA
JSHW012018250523
42278JS00005B/290